EVERY PARENT'S
Self-Help
Workbook

Carol Markie-Dadds MPsychClin
Matthew R. Sanders PhD
Karen M. T. Turner MPsychClin

Published by
Families International Publishing Pty Ltd ABN 17 079 825 817
PO Box 1300
Milton QLD 4064
Website: www.triplep.net

First published 1999

Reprinted 2000
         2001
         2002
         2003
         2005

Every Parent's Self-Help Workbook (Edition II)

Copyright © 2001   The University of Queensland

ISBN 1 876426 04 7

Designed and typeset in Goudy 10.5/12.5 by Australian Academic Press, Brisbane.

Cover and text design by Andrea Cox

Cartoons by Heck Lindsay

Contents

Acknowledgments

The Positive Parenting Program (Triple P) is an initiative of the Parenting and Family Support Centre at The University of Queensland. Triple P is dedicated to the many parents and children who have participated in the development of the program. Many of the ideas and principles of positive parenting contained in this volume have evolved as a result of the experience and feedback provided by parents and children participating in research and therapy programs. Their assistance is gratefully acknowledged. The authors also gratefully acknowledge the financial support of Queensland Health, Victorian Department of Human Services, Health Department of Western Australia, the National Health and Medical Research Council of Australia, and the School of Psychology and Department of Psychiatry at The University of Queensland who have contributed to the development of Triple P over the years.

About the Authors

Carol Markie-Dadds Carol Markie-Dadds is a clinical psychologist with Masters of Clinical Psychology from The University of Queensland. Carol is a Principal Policy Officer with the Queensland State Government. She is involved in coordinating and undertaking research and assessing strategic initiatives occurring at state, national and international levels that have implications for the delivery of educational services in Queensland. She has specialist clinical and research experience in working with families of young children with behavior problems.

Matthew R. Sanders is the Director of the Parenting and Family Support Centre at The University of Queensland and a Professor in Clinical Psychology. Over the past 25 years, Matt has gained an international reputation for scientific research into childhood behaviour problems and family intervention. He has written numerous articles on child and family intervention for scientific journals, and authored several books on the treatment of children's behaviour problems. He is past National President of the Australian Association of Cognitive Behaviour Therapy (AACBT), and in 1996 won a Distinguished Career Award from the AACBT.

Karen Turner is the Triple P Clinic Director and Program Development Coordinator at the Parenting and Family Support Centre. She is a clinical psychologist with a Masters degree in Clinical Psychology from The University of Queensland. Her work involves the management of an outpatient clinic and training facility, program development, public relations and consultancy projects for state and federal government departments and private sector initiatives. She has extensive clinical and research experience relating to the treatment of a variety of childhood behavioural and emotional problems.

Introduction

The Positive Parenting Program (Triple P) aims to make parenting easier. This workbook offers suggestions and ideas on positive parenting to help you promote your child's development.

Parenthood can be extremely rewarding, enlightening and enjoyable. It can also be demanding, frustrating and exhausting. Parents have the important role of raising the next generation, yet most people begin their careers as parents with little preparation, and learn through trial and error. The challenge for all parents is to raise healthy, well-adjusted children in a loving, predictable environment.

There is no single right way to be a parent and there are many different views on how parents should go about raising their children. Ultimately, you as the parent need to develop your own approach to dealing with your child's behaviour. Triple P has been helpful for many parents and may give you some useful ideas to help you meet the challenges of raising children.

We hope that you will find this program useful in undertaking the most important and rewarding job in our society — raising the next generation.

How To Use This Workbook

This workbook can be used alone or in conjunction with a number of Triple P resource materials. Each week, you will be asked to read sections of your workbook and complete several associated exercises. An Answers to Exercises section is included in this workbook to help you complete exercises designed to help you plan how to use positive parenting strategies with your family. Additional recommended resource materials are also listed for each week of the program.

Self-Help Triple P has been designed to make sure you have the necessary information and skills needed to practise positive parenting strategies as soon as possible. This means you may find that some weeks have a larger amount of reading and perhaps a few more exercises to complete than other weeks. The exercises have been designed to help you use suggested strategies with your own family. Each week, you will be asked to practise some of the skills introduced in your workbook. This is to give you an opportunity to try out for yourself whether the ideas suggested are for you. To get the most out of the program it is important that you make a commitment to doing these practice exercises.

The program has been designed to be completed once a week for 10 weeks. It is best to work through the recommended readings and associated exercises in your workbook at the same time. Try to avoid reading large sections of text and then tackling all the workbook exercises at once. In two-parent families, it is recommended that both parents complete this program. However, if this is not possible, the program can be successfully completed by the major caregiver.

Triple P Resource Materials

Triple P Tip Sheet Series

The *Positive Parenting* booklet accompanies a series of parenting tip sheets designed to give parents practical information and advice on positive approaches to parenting. The ideas in this booklet can be used to promote healthy development in children and to deal with a wide variety of common behaviour difficulties and developmental concerns. The individual tip sheets in the Triple P series will be most useful if you first become familiar with the ideas contained in the *Positive Parenting* booklet or *Every Parent's Self-Help Workbook*. After reading this material, refer to the individual tip sheets for infants, toddlers, preschoolers, primary schoolers and general parenting issues.

Every Parent Video Series

You may also find it useful to view a companion video, *Every Parent's Survival Guide* which illustrates each positive parenting strategy.

Other videos in the series are:

- *Every Parent's Guide to Infants and Toddlers*
- *Every Parent's Guide to Preschoolers*
- *Every Parent's Guide to Primary Schoolers*

Each video in this series clearly describes and explains how to prevent and overcome a variety of specific concerns for children in each age group.

Every Parent Video Series

A further series of videos exploring specific problems is available. Titles include:

- *Self-Esteem*
- *Children and Sport*
- *Encouraging Creativity*
- *Dealing with Disobedience*
- *Tidying Up*
- *Coping with Stress*
- *Supporting Your Partner*

Where To Find These Resources

Ask for the *Triple P Tip Sheets*, *Every Parent Video Series* and *Triple P Video Series* at your local childcare centre, kindergarten, preschool or primary school or at your local community health centre or library.

Your Commitment

This program is designed to support you in your parenting role. It will require your commitment, your partnership, your time and your full participation if it is to achieve its aim. If you work through the program, you will be rewarded. As you begin reading and completing the exercises that follow, you will learn new skills and possibly new ways of thinking, acting and organising your life. If you practise these new skills and keep up your level of motivation, the program will be of more benefit to you. So, before beginning, carefully consider your level of commitment or determination to complete this program. Below you will find a declaration of commitment to complete. This declaration is simply an agreement you make with yourself to see the program through to completion.

I (name) _____ agree to play an active role throughout the program. I am able to… (please tick the boxes corresponding to the aspects of the program you are able to take part in)

☐ set aside 1 hour or more a week to work through the program

☐ complete the readings and exercises

☐ complete the practice exercises suggested

Signed: _____ Date: _____

Witness: _____

I (name) _____ agree to play an active role throughout the program. I am able to… (please tick the boxes corresponding to the aspects of the program you are able to take part in)

☐ set aside 1 hour or more a week to work through the program

☐ complete the readings and exercises

☐ complete the practice exercises suggested

Signed: _____ Date: _____

Witness: _____

Now that you have decided to participate, we wish you well and hope that you find the program helpful and informative.

Overview of Self-Help Triple P

WEEK	TOPICS COVERED
1	• What is positive parenting? • Causes of child behaviour problems • Goals for change • Keeping track of children's behaviour
2	• Developing positive relationships with children • Encouraging desirable behaviour • Teaching new skills and behaviours
3	• Managing misbehaviour • Developing parenting routines • Finalising your behaviour chart
4	• Designing a practice task • Monitoring your implementation of strategies • Reviewing your performance
5	• Designing a practice task • Monitoring your implementation of strategies • Reviewing your performance
6	• Designing a practice task • Monitoring your implementation of strategies • Reviewing your performance
7	• Family survival tips • High risk situations • Planned activities routines
8	• Review of planned activities routines • Further planning
9	• Review of planned activities routines • Further planning
10	• Review of planned activities routines • Phasing out the program • Update on progress • Maintaining changes • Future goals

Positive Parenting

OVERVIEW

During Week 1 you will be given an introduction to the aims of Triple P and what the program involves. There will be an opportunity for you to think about some of your experiences and ideas about being a parent. You will be introduced to positive parenting as an approach to raising children. You will then look at factors that influence children's behaviour, set goals for change and start to keep track of your child's behaviour.

OBJECTIVES

By the end of Week 1, you should be able to:

- Describe positive parenting and what it involves.
- Identify factors that play a role in your child's behaviour patterns.
- Set goals for change in your child's and your own behaviour.
- Start monitoring one or two of your child's behaviours.

EXERCISE **1** *What you would like to get out of the program*

> Think about why you are participating in Self-Help Triple P and what you hope to get out of this experience. Jot down your ideas in the space below.
>
> ....
>
> ....
>
> ....
>
> ....

You may be participating in Self-Help Triple P to get some suggestions on how to cope with challenging child behaviour such as aggression, disobedience or destructiveness. You may be looking for solutions to some common, everyday parenting concerns such as taking children shopping, encouraging children to help out around the house or getting children to sleep in their own bed all night. You may simply be interested in finding out about positive parenting strategies for promoting your child's development. Whatever your reasons for participating in the program, we congratulate you for coming this far and hope that both you and your child benefit from the program in some very practical ways.

What is Positive Parenting?

Positive parenting is an approach to parenting that aims to promote children's development and manage children's behaviour in a constructive and non-hurtful way. It is based on good communication and positive attention to help children develop. Children who grow up with positive parenting are likely to develop their skills and feel good about themselves. They are also less likely to develop behaviour problems. There are five key aspects to positive parenting.

Ensuring a safe, interesting environment

Young children need a safe play environment, particularly once they begin to crawl. Accidents in the home are a leading cause of injury in young children. Having a safe environment means that you can be more relaxed about parenting and your child can explore and keep busy throughout the day with less risk of being hurt.

Children need an interesting environment that provides plenty of opportunities to explore, discover, experiment and develop their skills. A home that is full of interesting things to do will stimulate your child's curiosity as well as their language and intellectual development. It will also keep your child engaged and active and reduce the likelihood of misbehaviour.

Children also need to be adequately supervised. Adequate supervision means knowing where your child is and what they are doing at all times.

Creating a positive learning environment

Parents need to be available to their children. This does not mean being with your child all the time, but it means being available when your child needs help, care or attention. When your child approaches you, stop what you are doing and spend time with your child if you can.

Help your child learn by encouraging them to try things for themselves. Encouragement and positive attention help motivate children to learn. When you see your child doing something that you like, pay attention. Show your child that you like what they are doing and they will be more likely to do it again.

Using assertive discipline

Assertive discipline involves being consistent, acting quickly when children misbehave and teaching children to behave in an acceptable way. When parents use assertive discipline, children learn to accept responsibility for their behaviour, to become aware of the needs of others, and to develop self-control. Children are also less likely to develop behaviour problems if their parents are consistent and predictable from one day to the next.

You can value your child's individuality and still expect reasonable behaviour. When your child is misbehaving or upset, it is best to remain calm and avoid yelling, name calling, threatening or smacking.

Having realistic expectations

Parents' expectations of their child depend on what they consider normal for children at different ages. Remember, children are individuals and develop at different rates. Children need to be developmentally ready before they can learn new skills, such as using the toilet, dressing or feeding themselves. If you are unsure whether your child is ready to learn a new skill, seek professional advice.

Problems may arise when parents expect too much too soon, or expect their children to be perfect. For example, parents who expect that their child will *always* be polite, happy and cooperative or *always* tidy and helpful are setting themselves up for disappointment and conflict with their children. Do not expect your child to be perfect. All children make mistakes. Most mistakes are not intentional.

It is also important for parents to have realistic expectations of themselves. It is good to want to do your best as a parent, but trying to be a *perfect* parent will only lead to feelings of frustration and inadequacy. Do not be too hard on yourself. Everyone learns through experience.

Taking care of yourself as a parent

Parenting is easier when personal needs for intimacy, companionship, recreation and time alone are being met. Being a good parent does not mean that your child should dominate your life. If your own needs as an adult are being met, it is much easier to be patient, consistent and available to your child.

EXERCISE 2 *What is positive parenting?*

Which of these positive parenting skills do you find easy? Why?

....

....

....

....

Which of these skills do you find difficult? Why?

....

....

....

....

What other things are important in helping children develop?

....

....

....

....

Every Parent's Self-Help Workbook

Causes of Child Behaviour Problems

Why do children behave as they do? How is it that children from the same family can be so alike in some ways and so different in others? To understand how children's behaviour develops, we need to consider three things — their genetic make-up, their family environment and the community in which they live. These factors shape the skills, attitudes and abilities children develop and also influence whether they develop behaviour problems.

EXERCISE 3 *Identifying causes of child behaviour problems*

Children behave in both desirable and undesirable ways for a reason. By understanding these reasons, we can look at what changes we need to make in both our child's and our own behaviour to prevent behaviour problems. In this next exercise, the aim is for you to get an understanding of what it is that might be going on in your family that could influence your child's behaviour. Since you know your child better than anyone else, you are the expert. As you read through the following section which presents some possible causes of behaviour problems, ask yourself three questions: Does this apply to my child? Which factors are most important in explaining my child's behaviour? Is there anything else I think is important that is not on the list? You may also like to include some comments in the spaces provided.

For two-parent families, it is important for each parent to focus on themselves rather than on their partner. Avoid blaming your partner for your child's behaviour patterns. Try to focus on your own parenting styles.

GENETIC MAKE-UP

Children inherit a unique genetic make-up from their parents. This may include physical characteristics, such as eye colour and hair texture, as well as some behavioural and emotional characteristics. For example, children who have problems concentrating or who have a tendency to feel sad or depressed may have inherited a genetic make-up that makes them more likely to have these problems.

Children may also inherit their temperament from their parents, such as how sociable or outgoing they are, how active they are, or how emotional they are. Some of these characteristics can make children difficult to manage. For example, some children demand a lot of attention, others are very active or busy and constantly explore their surroundings, others cry and fuss a lot and are difficult to settle into feeding and sleeping routines. However, not all difficult babies develop behaviour problems as children, and some easy babies do. Children's behaviour depends not only on their temperament but on how others react to their behaviour.

What was your child like as an infant?

- liked to be with people, demanded lots of attention ☐
- easily upset, difficult to settle, distressed by sudden change ☐
- very active, busy, energetic, difficult to control ☐

Comments:

....

....

....

THE FAMILY ENVIRONMENT

Children's genetic make-up is something that cannot be changed. However, children learn from their family environment, and this can be changed to teach them to behave in a more appropriate way. Understanding how children learn from their environment is useful in deciding how to deal with problems.

Accidental rewards for misbehaviour

Children quickly learn that their behaviour has an effect and they can control the actions of others. Problem behaviour is likely to continue if it gets children what they want. Often there are accidental rewards or hidden pay-offs for misbehaviour. Accidental rewards include social attention (such as talking, a wink or a smile), material rewards (such as toys), activities (such as a parent distracting their child with a game) or food treats (such as biscuits, ice-cream or lollies). For example, if you accidentally laugh or spend a lot of time reasoning with your child the first time they say a swear word, the extra attention may encourage your child to swear again.

Do any of these accidental rewards occur in your family?

- social attention ☐
- material rewards ☐
- activity rewards ☐
- food rewards ☐

Comments:

....

....

....

....

Escalation traps

Children can learn that if they escalate and their problem behaviour gets worse, they are more likely to get what they want. For example, your child may ask for a biscuit just before dinner. You may say *No* several times. However, if your child persists and gets louder and more demanding, you may fall into the trap of giving them a biscuit just to stop the noise. Unfortunately, your child is rewarded for becoming more demanding and learns to persist and get louder to get their own way. You are rewarded because your child stops making noise, at least in the short term. Since both you and your child are rewarded, this escalation is likely to occur again.

In a similar way, parents can learn that if they escalate and get louder, they are more likely to get what they want. For example, you may give an instruction to your child several times, gradually getting louder without any success. Eventually, you may angrily demand that your child does as you ask before you have counted to three, *or else!* Your child then learns that you are only serious when you yell and count, and will wait until then before they do as you ask. You are rewarded for yelling as your child does as you ask and your child is rewarded because you stop yelling at them. Again, since there is a pay-off for both you and your child, this escalation is likely to happen again.

Do either of these escalation traps occur in your family?

- child escalates ☐
- parent escalates ☐

Comments:

....

....

....

Ignoring desirable behaviour

For some children there is little or no pay-off for good behaviour. Unfortunately, behaviour that earns no attention is likely to happen less often. If children are ignored when they behave well, they may learn that the only way to get attention is to misbehave.

Do you often fall into this trap?

● ignoring desirable behaviour ☐

Comments:

....

....

....

Watching others

Children learn by watching what other people do. For example, when parents get angry and yell at others, and get their own way because they yell, children learn that it is alright to shout when they have a problem. Children whose parents smack often are likely to hit a lot as well. Behaviours such as yelling, talking back, losing your temper, swearing, hitting, untidiness and how to react when something frightening happens, can all be learnt through watching others.

Does your child pick up any bad habits from watching others?

● watching others ☐

Comments:

....

....

....

Giving instructions

The way in which parents give instructions can influence whether or not children do as they are told. Some common problems include:

● *Too many.* Every time an instruction is given there is an opportunity for children to be disobedient. Children can feel picked on when they are given too many instructions.

● *Too few.* Children sometimes seem disobedient because no-one has taken the time to give them clear instructions about what is expected. For example, a child may have poor table manners because they have not been given enough instructions on how to use a knife and fork.

● *Too hard.* Children may be disobedient when parents expect too much and give instructions that are beyond their child's abilities, such as asking a 3-year-old to tidy up a very messy room.

● *Poorly timed.* Instructions given when a child is busy doing something, such as watching a favourite television show, are likely to be ignored.

- *Too vague*. Children may not follow instructions that are unclear — *Denise!...* or *Don't be silly* — or instructions that are expressed as questions — *Would you like to go to bed now?* If you give your child a choice, be prepared for them to say *No*.
- *Body language*. Sometimes a parent's body language says something different to the instruction, such as laughing or smiling while telling a child to stop what they are doing. This can confuse children. Also, children often ignore instructions shouted from one room to another, because parents are not there to back up the instruction.

How do you give instructions?

- too many ☐
- too few ☐
- too hard ☐
- poorly timed ☐
- too vague ☐
- confusing body language ☐

Comments:

....

....

....

....

Emotional messages

Parents who disapprove of their child rather than their child's behaviour may lower their child's self-esteem. Calling children names — *stupid* or *idiot* — and guilt-inducing messages — *What would Grandma think if she could see you carrying on like this?* — may shame children into cooperating. However, this can make children angry, resentful and uncooperative.

Do you give any of these emotional messages?

- name calling or put downs ☐
- guilt-inducing messages ☐

Comments:

....

....

....

....

Ineffective use of punishment

Children can develop behaviour problems because of the way parents use punishment or discipline. Here are some reasons why punishment does not work.

- *Punishment threatened but not carried out.* Although threats may work at first, children quickly learn to ignore instructions when parents do not follow through with their threats. Threats of punishment can even serve as a dare, and children may test their parents just to see what happens.
- *Punishment given in anger.* There is always a risk of losing control and hurting a child when parents give punishment in anger. Seek professional help if you are worried that this might happen.
- *Punishment as a crisis response.* Sometimes parents overreact to misbehaviour because they wait until their child's behaviour is unbearable before doing something about it.
- *Inconsistent use of punishment.* Inconsistency makes it difficult for children to learn what is expected of them. Behaviour problems can arise when instructions and rules are not consistently applied from day to day. In two-parent families, problems can also arise when parents contradict each other or do not back each other up in front of the children.

Do you have any of these difficulties with discipline?

- threats not carried out ☐
- punishment given in anger ☐
- punishment as a crisis response ☐
- inconsistent use of punishment ☐

Comments:

....

....

....

....

Parents' beliefs and expectations

Some beliefs are unhelpful and can make parenting difficult. Here are some common unhelpful beliefs.

- *It's just a phase.* This belief can stop parents from dealing with problem behaviour straight away. Instead, parents may wait until a problem is severe and long standing before seeking help or making changes.
- *He's doing it deliberately, just to annoy me.* This belief places blame on the child and may make parents resentful, leading them to overreact to misbehaviour. It may also stop parents from looking at how their own actions contribute to the problem behaviour.

- *It's all my fault she's the way she is.* This belief blames parents for children's problem behaviour. Parents may feel guilty and depressed if they think they are to blame for their child's behaviour. This makes it even harder to be patient, calm and consistent with their children.

Parents' expectations can also make parenting more difficult. It is unrealistic for parents to expect their children to be perfect. This is likely to lead to disappointment and conflict with their children. Parents can also have unrealistic expectations of themselves. When parents aim to do a perfect job, they are setting themselves up for dissatisfaction and frustration.

Do either of these apply to you?

- unhelpful beliefs ☐
- unrealistic expectations ☐

Comments:

....

....

....

Other influences on the family

There are other influences on parents' well-being that can make parenting more difficult. Here are some examples:

- *Parents' relationship.* Problem behaviour can occur when a couple's relationship is strained and there is tension and conflict in the home. Boys may become aggressive and girls may become anxious or depressed when they see a lot of arguments and fights between their parents.

- *Parents' emotions*. Parents' feelings, such as anger, depression or anxiety, can prevent them from being consistent and managing their children's behaviour effectively. For example, if a parent is feeling sad or depressed, they are likely to be irritable and impatient, have unhelpful thoughts about their child, want to spend less time with their child and provide less supervision.
- *Stress*. All parents experience stresses at some time, such as moving house, financial problems and work pressures. Children need routine and may become upset if these stresses disrupt the usual family routine for a long period of time.

Do any of these apply to your family?

- parents' relationship with each other ☐
- parents' feelings ☐
- stress ☐

Comments:

....

....

....

....

INFLUENCES OUTSIDE THE HOME

It is not possible for parents to control all influences on their child's behaviour. Children's behaviour is also influenced by factors outside the home, once they have more contact with others in the community.

Peers and friends

When children start to mix with other children, they are influenced by their relationships with peers and by what other children do. For example, aggressive and disruptive children are often rejected by their peers, have poor social skills and find it hard to make and keep friends. It is likely that these children will mix with and learn from other disruptive children and the problem behaviour will continue.

School

Children's success at school can influence their adjustment and behaviour. For example, a child may develop behaviour problems because they find school work difficult, do not do well and rarely receive any praise or rewards for their efforts.

Media and technology

Children can learn problem behaviour, such as swearing or aggression, from watching movies and television programs, reading newspapers and comics, or playing computer games.

Are any of these a concern for your family?

- peers and friends ☐
- school ☐
- media and technology ☐

Comments:

....

....

....

....

All parents can fall into parenting traps at times. You would probably need to be super-human to raise your child without ever giving an accidental reward or falling into an escalation trap or being inconsistent. Really it is not possible to be a parent without making some mistakes along the way. However, child behaviour problems are more likely to occur if you find you are often falling into these parenting traps. So, how often these day to day interactions occur is far more important than simply whether or not they occur.

Other Factors

Are you aware of any other things that could be influencing your child's behaviour? If so, list them in the space below.

....

....

....

....

Goals for Change

Now that you have looked at the possible causes of behaviour problems, think about changes you would like to see in your child's behaviour, as well as in your own.

It is up to you, the parent, to decide what skills to teach your child. Remember, children must be developmentally ready before they learn a new skill. It may be helpful to have in mind the skills that help children learn to be independent and to get along with others.

EXERCISE 4 *What skills should we encourage in children?*

Look at the list below and think about skills you would like to encourage in your child.

How to communicate and get on with others

- Expressing their views, ideas and needs appropriately.
- Requesting assistance or help when they need it.
- Cooperating with adult requests.
- Playing cooperatively with other children.
- Being aware of the feelings of others.
- Being aware of how their own actions affect others.

How to manage their feelings

- Expressing feelings in ways that do not harm others.
- Controlling hurtful actions and thinking before acting.
- Developing positive feelings about themselves and others.
- Accepting rules and limits.

How to be independent

- Doing things for themselves.
- Keeping busy without constant adult attention.
- Being responsible for their own actions.

How to solve problems

- Showing an interest and curiosity in everyday things.
- Asking questions and developing ideas.
- Considering alternative solutions.
- Negotiating and compromising.
- Making decisions and solving problems for themselves.

Comments:

....

....

....

....

EXERCISE 5 *Setting goals for change*

It is now time to start thinking about goals for change. It is important to set goals at the start of Self-Help Triple P. This way you will know what you are working towards and whether you are making progress. When developing your goals for change, consider your child's behaviour now. Think of what you would like your child to do more often (e.g. speak politely, play by themselves without constant adult attention, do as they are told, stay in their own bed all night). Also consider what you would like your child to do less often (e.g. tantrum, fight, complain during meals, interrupt). It is also important to think about what changes you would like to make in your own behaviour. Now that you have looked at what may contribute to your child's problem behaviour, set yourself some goals. Consider what you would like to do more often (e.g. stay calm, give clear, direct instructions), and what you would like to do less often (e.g. use threats, shout instructions from another room).

> In the space below, list those changes that you would like to see in your child's behaviour and your own behaviour. Make sure your goals are specific and achievable.

GOALS FOR CHANGE IN YOUR CHILD'S BEHAVIOUR	GOALS FOR CHANGE IN YOUR OWN BEHAVIOUR

Keeping Track of Children's Behaviour

To help you know how close you are getting to achieving your goals, it is useful to keep track of your child's and your own behaviour. Keeping a record is helpful for many reasons.

- It gives you a chance to check out whether what you think about your child's behaviour is actually true (e.g. does your child throw a tantrum every time you go out?).
- It helps you monitor your own reactions to your child's behaviour and identify when and why the behaviour occurs.
- It allows you to assess whether the behaviour is changing (i.e. improving, worsening or staying the same).
- It tells you when you have achieved your goal.

A number of monitoring forms are available for helping you keep track of your child's behaviour.

Behaviour diary

Keeping a behaviour diary involves writing down when and where a problem behaviour occurred, what happened before the problem behaviour (what caused it) and what happened afterwards (how you reacted). This will help you to identify:

- patterns in your child's behaviour
- how often the behaviour occurs
- how consistently you deal with your child's behaviour
- high-risk times or situations
- possible triggers or causes
- possible accidental rewards

Use this form for behaviours that occur less than five times per day. For behaviours that occur more often, choose another recording form. You may like to also use this form for one or two examples each day of a behaviour that occurs often. An example behaviour diary for one day is shown on page 17.

Instructions: List the problem behaviour, when and where it occurred and what happened before and after the event.

Problem Behaviour: Tantrums   Day: Friday, May 14th

PROBLEM EVENT	WHEN AND WHERE DID IT OCCUR?	WHAT OCCURRED BEFORE THE EVENT?	WHAT OCCURRED AFTER THE EVENT?	OTHER COMMENTS
Rolling on floor, crying	7.30 a.m. Family room	Asked to get dressed	Allowed to watch TV a bit longer	
Kicking feet on floor, yelling	8.00 a.m. Family room	Turned TV off told to get dressed	Carried to room Helped to dress	Late leaving house, angry
Shouting, yelling, stamping feet	10.30 a.m Supermarket	Not allowed to have new toy	Gave in and bought it	Embarrassed, anything for quiet!
Shouting, hitting fists on floor	12.30 p.m. Family room	Asked to tidy up toys before lunch	Sent to room Tidied up myself	Screamed for 35 minutes in room
Pouting, crying loudly	6.00 p.m. Outside	Told to finish game and come to dinner	Smacked, sent to room, no dinner	Guilty, TV and ice-cream later

Tally sheet

Another way to keep track of your child's behaviour is to write down how often it occurs. To do this, on a tally sheet like the one below, mark off each time the behaviour occurs during the day.

Use this form for behaviours that occur up to 15 times per day. For behaviours that occur more often, choose another recording form.

EXAMPLE TALLY SHEET

Instructions: Write the day in the first column, then place a tick in the successive square each time the problem behaviour occurs on that day. Record the total number of episodes for each day in the end column.

Starting Date: October 17th

Behaviour: Swearing

DAY	1	2	3	4	5	6	7	8	9	10	11	12	13	14	15	TOTAL
Sun	✓	✓	✓	✓	✓	✓	✓	✓	✓							9
Mon	✓	✓	✓	✓	✓	✓	✓	✓	✓	✓	✓					11
Tues	✓	✓	✓	✓	✓	✓	✓	✓								8

Duration record

This is a useful form for tracking how long a behaviour lasts such as how long an infant cries during the day, or how long a child spends completing their homework or getting ready for school in the morning. Simply time how long each instance of the target behaviour lasts in seconds, minutes or hours and write this on the chart. At the end of each day, add up the time of each episode to see the total amount of time the behaviour lasted. An example duration record is included below.

Use this form when you want to know how long a behaviour lasts. For behaviours that come and go quickly or often, use a time sample form, otherwise use a behaviour diary or tally sheet.

EXAMPLE DURATION RECORD

Instructions: Write the day in the first column, then for each separate occurrence of the target behaviour, record how long it lasted in seconds, minutes or hours. Total the times at the end of each day.

Behaviour: Crying after put to bed   **Starting Date:** February 8th

DAY	SUCCESSIVE EPISODES										TOTAL
	1	2	3	4	5	6	7	8	9	10	
Mon	30 min	20 min									50 min
Tues	10 min	15 min	12 min								37 min
Wed	5 min	15 min	8 min								28 min
Thurs	20 min	10 min	12 min	20 min							62 min

Time sample

This form is useful for tracking behaviours that occur more than several times an hour, such as whining, complaining or disobedience. It is best to pick a high-risk time of the day to complete this form. Choose a 2–3 hour time period when the target behaviour is more likely to occur, such as in the morning before school or in the late afternoon before dinner. Once you have identified a high-risk time, break this period into 15 or 30 minute time blocks. To complete the form, put a mark in the square if the target behaviour occurred at least once during the time interval.

Use this form for behaviours that occur often (more than 10 or 15 times per day), behaviours that come and go quickly and often over a short period of time, or behaviours that do not have a clear beginning and end. Choose another recording form for behaviours that occur less often.

EXAMPLE TIME SAMPLE

Instructions: Place a tick in the square for the corresponding time period if the target behaviour has occurred at least once.

Behaviour: Whining   **Starting Date:** April 5th

TIME OF DAY — THIRTY MINUTE INTERVALS

Time	M	T	W	T	F	S	S	M	T	W	T	F	S	S	M	T	W
9.00 am – 9.30 am																	
9.30 am – 10.00 am																	
10.00 am – 10.30 am																	
10.30 am – 11.00 am																	
11.00 am – 11.30 am																	
11.30 am – 12.00 noon																	
12.00 noon – 12.30 pm																	
12.30 pm – 1.00 pm																	
1.00 pm – 1.30 pm																	
1.30 pm – 2.00 pm																	
2.00 pm – 2.30 pm																	
2.30 pm – 3.00 pm																	
3.00 pm – 3.30 pm																	
3.30 pm – 4.00 pm																	
4.00 pm – 4.30 pm			✔	✔	✔	✔											
4.30 pm – 5.00 pm		✔	✔	✔	✔		✔										
5.00 pm – 5.30 pm		✔	✔														
5.30 pm – 6.00 pm	✔	✔	✔	✔		✔	✔										
6.00 pm – 6.30 pm	✔	✔		✔		✔	✔										
6.30 pm – 7.00 pm	✔	✔	✔	✔	✔	✔											
DAYS	M	T	W	T	F	S	S	M	T	W	T	F	S	S	M	T	W
TOTAL	3	5	5	5	3	4	3										

Behaviour graph

You can put the information you collect on a graph to make it easier to keep track of your child's progress (see below). Keep track like this for a week or so before you start a new parenting plan. After you start a new parenting plan, continue to keep track of your child's behaviour to see whether your new plan is successful. This will help you notice improvements in your child's behaviour and keep you motivated to continue using new strategies or routines.

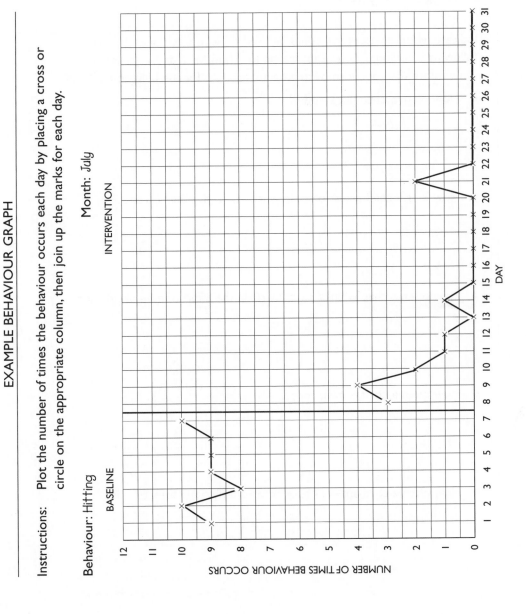

EXAMPLE BEHAVIOUR GRAPH

Instructions: Plot the number of times the behaviour occurs each day by placing a cross or circle on the appropriate column, then join up the marks for each day.

Month: July

Behaviour: Hitting

BASELINE

INTERVENTION

NUMBER OF TIMES BEHAVIOUR OCCURS

DAY

When you start a new parenting plan, it is useful to have a trial period of around 7–10 days. At the end of the trial period, you can decide whether to keep going in the same way or make minor changes to your plan. Remember, the best way to change children's behaviour, and your own, is to do it gradually. Once new routines or behaviours are well established you can keep track less often, such as once a week instead of daily. Stop recording completely when you are confident of your progress. If you are concerned about your progress, seek professional help.

EXERCISE 6 *Keeping track*

Indicate which type of form could be used to keep track of each of the following behaviours. Give your reason for choosing a particular form. Often more than one form would be appropriate for the behaviours listed.

- How often a child bites others.

  ....

  ....

  ....

- How long a child takes to settle when left with other carers.

  ....

  ....

  ....

- How often a child whines, particularly in the afternoon before dinner.

  ....

  ....

  ....

- How often a child is destructive.

  ....

  ....

  ....

- How often a child answers back or uses a negative tone of voice.

  ....

  ....

  ....

Summary of Activities

Week 1 has looked at what positive parenting involves and some causes of children's behaviour problems. You have thought about the skills and behaviours you would like to encourage in your child and set some goals for change. To finish, you have looked at some ways of keeping track of your child's behaviour.

■ PRACTICE EXERCISES

- Select one or two of your child's problem behaviours for monitoring. Keep track of these behaviours for 7 days using a monitoring form from pages 24–27 (additional copies of these forms can be found in the Worksheets section). After 7 days, plot your data onto a behaviour graph (page 28). Jot down the behaviour/s you plan to track for the next 7 days. Which type of monitoring form will you use?

■ OPTIONAL HOMEWORK

For a review of the material covered in today's session, you may like to watch:

- *Every Parent's Survival Guide*, Part 1, What is Positive Parenting?
- *Every Parent's Survival Guide*, Part 2, Causes of Child Behaviour Problems, Goals for Change, Keeping Track

Content of Next Week

Week 2 will look at practical strategies for:

- Building positive relationships with children.
- Encouraging desirable behaviour.
- Teaching children new skills and behaviours.

Week 1

BEHAVIOUR DIARY

Instructions: List the problem behaviour, when and where it occurred and what happened before and after the event.

Problem Behaviour: _____

Day: _____

PROBLEM EVENT	WHEN AND WHERE DID IT OCCUR?	WHAT OCCURRED BEFORE THE EVENT?	WHAT OCCURRED AFTER THE EVENT?	OTHER COMMENTS

TALLY SHEET

Instructions: Write the day in the first column, then place a tick in the successive square each time the behaviour occurs on that day. Record the total number of episodes for each day in the end column.

Behaviour: _____

Starting Date: _____

DAY	1	2	3	4	5	6	7	8	9	10	11	12	13	14	15	TOTAL

Week 1

DURATION RECORD

Instructions: Write the day in the first column, then for each separate occurrence of the target behaviour, record how long it lasted in seconds, minutes or hours. Total the times at the end of each day.

Behaviour: _____   Starting Date: _____

DAY	SUCCESSIVE EPISODES										TOTAL
	1	2	3	4	5	6	7	8	9	10	

TIME SAMPLE

Instructions: Place a tick in the square for the corresponding time period if the target behaviour has occurred at least once.

Behaviour: _____   Starting Date: _____

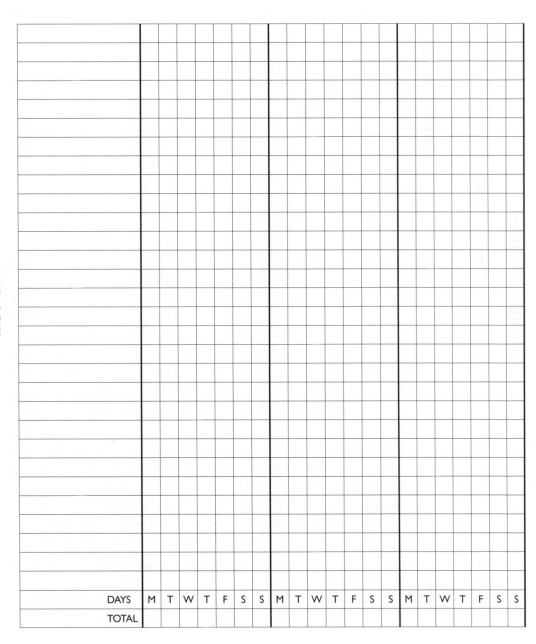

TIME OF DAY

DAYS	M	T	W	T	F	S	S	M	T	W	T	F	S	S	M	T	W	T	F	S	S
TOTAL																					

■ **PRACTICE EXERCISES** ***Monitoring form 5***

BEHAVIOUR GRAPH

Instructions: Plot the number of times the behaviour occurs each day by placing a cross or circle in the appropriate column, then join up the marks for each day.

Behaviour: ____________________ Month: ____________

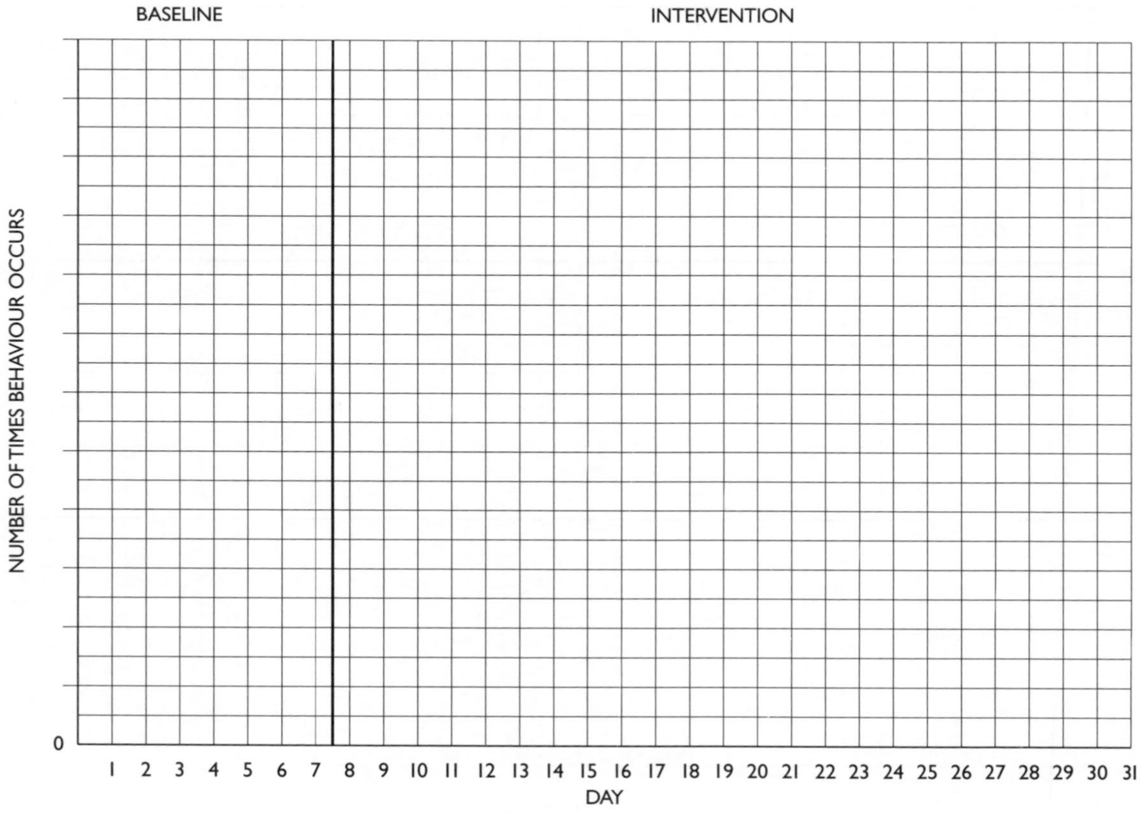

BASELINE
INTERVENTION
NUMBER OF TIMES BEHAVIOUR OCCURS
0
1 2 3 4 5 6 7 8 9 10 11 12 13 14 15 16 17 18 19 20 21 22 23 24 25 26 27 28 29 30 31
DAY

Promoting Children's Development

OVERVIEW

Encouragement and positive attention help children develop their skills and learn appropriate ways of behaving. Encouraging the behaviour you like increases the chances of the behaviour happening again. In Week 1, you decided on the behaviours and skills you would like to encourage in your child. This week, you will be introduced to a number of strategies that can help you promote your child's development by enhancing your relationship with your child, encouraging your child for desirable behaviour and teaching your child new skills. As you work through the exercises, think about the strategies you would feel most comfortable using with your child.

OBJECTIVES

By the end of Week 2, you should be able to:

- Use the strategies for developing a positive relationship with your child (i.e. quality time, talking with children, and showing affection).
- Use the strategies for encouraging desirable behaviour (i.e. praise, providing attention, and selecting age-appropriate, engaging activities for children).
- Use the strategies for teaching children new skills or behaviours (i.e. setting a good example, incidental teaching, and Ask, Say, Do).
- Choose two positive parenting strategies to practise and monitor for 7 days.
- Set up a behaviour chart with appropriate rewards for your child.

Promoting Children's Development

Before looking at how to manage misbehaviour, it is important to look at how to promote children's development and teach children to behave well. Many common behaviour problems can be solved by helping children learn better ways of handling situations they find difficult. As you work through the exercises for this week, think about what strategies you currently use with your child. You may have heard about and already use some of these strategies and some may be new to you. This week gives you a chance to think about your relationship with your child and whether you let them know when they are doing something that you like.

It is important to remember that all strategies have their limitations and no single strategy will work for all situations or in isolation. However, these strategies are the starting point for promoting your child's development and encouraging appropriate behaviour. Each of the strategies presented is intended to be used when children are behaving well rather than when they are uncooperative or misbehaving. Strategies for dealing with misbehaviour and teaching children self-control will be covered in Week 3.

Developing Positive Relationships With Children

All parents want to get on well with their children. Children develop their skills best when they have a warm, predictable and secure family environment. It takes time to form caring family relationships. Here are some ideas to help you develop a positive relationship with your child. As you work through Exercises 1 to 3, ask yourself what changes, if any, you feel you need to make to strengthen your relationship with your child.

Spend quality time with your child

Recommended age range: All ages. Spending frequent, small amounts of time with children can be more beneficial than less frequent longer periods of time. Try to spend small amounts of time with your child — as little as 1 or 2 minutes — frequently throughout the day. Time that is special to your child will occur when your child approaches you to tell you something, ask a question or involve you in their activity. When this happens, and you are not occupied with something important, stop what you are doing and make yourself available. If you are busy at the time, try to plan some time for your child as soon as you can.

EXERCISE 1 *Ideas for quality time*

> Quality time is different for all families. Write down some ideas about how
> you and your child can spend quality time together. Remember quality time
> is something that can happen every day, such as reading a story or playing a
> game, rather than special outings, such as trips to amusement parks.
>
> ....
>
> ....
>
> ....
>
> ....

Talk with your child

Recommended age range: All ages. Talking with your child helps them learn to
speak, teaches conversational and social skills and boosts your child's self-esteem.
Talk with your child about things they are interested in. Share ideas and information with your child and show that you are interested in what your child has to say.

EXERCISE 2 *Things to talk about*

> List some things that your child is interested in or that you have been doing
> that you can talk about.
>
> ....
>
> ....
>
> ....
>
> ....

Show affection

Recommended age range: All ages. Another way of showing you are interested and care for your child is to give them plenty of physical affection. Holding, touching, cuddling, kissing, massaging, tickling and hugging help children grow up feeling cared for and comfortable with giving and receiving affection. Affection in the first few years of a child's life helps them form secure bonds with their parents.

EXERCISE 3 *Ways to show affection*

What kind of physical affection do you and your child both enjoy?

....

....

....

....

Encouraging Desirable Behaviour

Children are more cooperative and less difficult to manage when they receive encouragement and positive attention for behaving well and when they have plenty of interesting and stimulating things to do. Here are some ideas you can use to encourage your child for behaving well. Remember, encouraging the behaviour you like increases the chance of that behaviour happening again. As you work through Exercises 4 to 6, ask yourself what changes, if any, you feel you need to make to encourage your child's desirable behaviour.

Praise your child

Recommended age range: All ages. All children, and adults, like to be praised. Notice your child behaving well and praise them for behaviour you like. Praise may be just stating your approval — *Good girl* or *Well done, that's great* — or a statement that describes exactly what you like — *Thanks for doing as I asked straight away* or *I'm really pleased you tidied up when you finished playing.* Avoid comments that bring up a problem behaviour — *It's good to see you two playing nicely for a change and not fighting* or *Thank you for not interrupting.* Descriptive praise is better than general approval for encouraging a particular behaviour that you like. Praise works best when you are enthusiastic and mean what you say.

EXERCISE 4 *How to give descriptive praise*

Look at your list of goals for things you would like your child to do more often (see page 15). Write down the goal behaviours and some praise statements you could use to encourage these goal behaviours. Try to be as specific and descriptive as you can.

....

....

....

....

....

....

Give your child attention

Recommended age range: All ages. There are many ways of giving attention. A smile, wink, pat on the back or just watching are all forms of attention that children enjoy and can be used to encourage behaviour you like. These actions add to your praise and show your child how pleased you are with their behaviour. You can also use these forms of attention to encourage your child for behaving well in situations where you are unable to praise them, such as when they are in a group of friends and your praise may embarrass them.

EXERCISE 5 *Ways to give attention*

Write down some ways you can give attention to your child.

....

....

....

....

Provide engaging activities

Recommended age range: All ages. Providing children with interesting and engaging activities encourages independent play. Environments that are safe and full of interesting things to do and explore, stimulate children's development and keep them busy. Provide your child with toys and activities, both at home and on outings. Toys and activities do not have to be expensive to be interesting and fun to your child.

EXERCISE 6 *Ideas for engaging activities*

Think of some fun new activities for your child. You may like to get some ideas from other parents. You may also be able to borrow some books on children's games from your local library, childcare centre, kindergarten or school. List some games and activities for indoors and outdoors.

INDOOR GAMES AND ACTIVITIES	OUTDOOR GAMES AND ACTIVITIES

Teaching New Skills and Behaviours

The next section looks at the role of parents as teachers. Growing up involves learning many new and complex skills such as brushing teeth, getting dressed, tidying up after yourself and strategies for solving problems. Parents need to know how to help their children learn these skills. Some suggestions are given on the following pages. As you work through Exercises 7 to 10, think about what changes, if any, you feel you need to make in helping your child learn new skills and behaviours.

Set a good example

Recommended age range: All ages. We all learn through watching others. To encourage new behaviours, let your child watch you. Describe what you are doing and let your child copy your actions. Provide help if necessary and encourage your child to try again without any help. Praise your child when they are successful.

Do not expect your child to follow house rules if no one else in the family does. For example, you cannot expect your child to follow house rules such as *Tidy up after yourself* if you leave your own things lying around. Set a good example to show your child how to behave.

EXERCISE 7 *Ways to set a good example*

> From your list of goals for your child's behaviour (on page 15), decide if there are any behaviours you can encourage by setting a good example. List them below.
>
> ....
>
> ....
>
> ....
>
> ....

Use incidental teaching

Recommended age range: 1–12 years. When children approach you for information, help or attention, they are often motivated and ready to learn. You are in a position to teach your child something new — this is called incidental teaching. Just telling your child the answer to a question does not help them learn to think for themselves. Prompt your child to come up with the answer and see if you can help them learn more — *What colour do you think it is? Yes it's red. What else is red?* This should be fun and enjoyable so do not push the issue. If your child does not respond, provide the answer and wait for another teaching opportunity.

EXERCISE 8 *Ideas for using incidental teaching*

There are different types of teaching opportunities that occur frequently. Think of how you could use incidental teaching in the following situations.

When your child asks you questions, particularly the common *Why?* questions (e.g. *Why is the moon round tonight?*).

....

....

....

When your child mispronounces a word (e.g. *sgetti* instead of *spaghetti*).

....

....

....

When your child is engaged in an activity and wants to show you something (e.g. *Come and look at my painting!*).

....

....

....

When your child is frustrated with an activity and asks for help (e.g. *I can't do this puzzle!*).

....

....

....

Use Ask, Say, Do

Recommended age range: 3–12 years. Ask, Say, Do is a good way to help your child learn to become independent in skills such as dressing, brushing their teeth or getting ready for bed. When a task is long and difficult, teach your child one step at a time. Follow these steps:

Ask

Ask your child what the first step is — *What is the first thing we do when we brush our teeth?*

Say

If your child does not give you the correct answer, calmly tell them what to do — *First, we put toothpaste on our brush. Now you show me how you put toothpaste on your brush.*

Do

If your child does not perform the task, help them. For example, open the toothpaste tube, put your hands over your child's hands and guide them through the task. Stop helping once the task is started to let your child finish by themselves.

Praise cooperation and success

Praise your child for cooperating and for any success at each step. Repeating what your child says or does is a good way of encouraging them — *That's right. We put toothpaste on the brush,* or *Good boy. That's great brushing.* As your child learns the new skill, you can use praise less often.

Repeat Ask, Say, Do for each step

Repeat this process for each step in the task, such as putting toothpaste on the brush, brushing teeth, rinsing and so on. Provide less help each time your child practises the task.

EXERCISE 9 *Ideas for using Ask, Say, Do*

Pick a behaviour or skill that you would like your child to learn to do by themselves, such as tying shoelaces, using the toilet or washing their body. Apply Ask, Say, Do to the first steps in the skill you want to teach. Here is an example of the first step for undressing and dressing:

Behaviour or Skill: *Undressing and dressing*

ASK	What is the first thing we do when we get dressed in the morning?
SAY	That's right, we take off our pyjama top
DO	Those buttons are hard to undo, I'll help you undo the first button

Now start on your Ask, Say, Do routine for the first three steps of your chosen task.

Behaviour or Skill: ....

ASK	
SAY	
DO	

ASK	
SAY	
DO	

ASK	
SAY	
DO	

Use behaviour charts

Recommended age range: 2–12 years. Sometimes children need a little extra motivation to change a behaviour, practise a new skill or complete set tasks. Behaviour charts are useful here. They are an effective short-term strategy that can be used for a few weeks and then phased out. Your child can earn stamps, stars, happy faces, stickers or points on a chart for desired behaviour. This gives your child a sense of achievement and recognition for their efforts.

A behaviour chart can be backed up by having a certain number of stamps or stickers earn a reward. Some of the best rewards involve activities, such as a family bike ride, special time with Mum or Dad, helping to bake a cake or going on a picnic. Other rewards include small treats like a lucky dip, choosing a video to hire, choosing dinner, a new book, magazine or small toy. Rewards may be negotiated with your child, ask what they would like to work for — within reason! Here is an example of a behaviour chart used to encourage a child to stay in their bed all night. You will notice that the rewards were made harder to achieve once the goal was being reached easily.

My happy faces chart for staying in my own bed all night

DAY 1	DAY 2	DAY 3	DAY 4	DAY 5	DAY 6	DAY 7
☺ reward	☺ reward		☺	☺ reward	☺	
DAY 8	DAY 9	DAY 10	DAY 11	DAY 12	DAY 13	DAY 14
☺ reward	☺	☺	☺		☺	☺ reward

Here are some guidelines for using a behaviour chart:

- Get ready all the things you will need. Draw up the chart (see example above). Obtain stickers, stars, or stamps.
- Describe the behaviour for which you are going to use a chart. State the behaviour positively, such as *Sitting up nicely at the dinner table* rather than *Not leaving the dinner table* or *Talking nicely* rather than *Not yelling*.
- Decide and explain how often your child can earn stickers or stamps.
- Set a goal for the number of stamps or stickers your child must earn before they receive a reward. Aim for an easy goal first so that your child has at least 2 days of success before the goal becomes harder to achieve. Ask your child to say the goal for earning stickers to be sure they understand.
- Decide on and explain the rewards your child can earn for a set number of stamps or stickers. Agree on practical rewards — not too expensive or difficult to organise.
- Decide on and explain the consequences for breaking a rule or failing to achieve the goal (see Week 3: Managing Misbehaviour).
- Praise your child each time they earn a stamp or sticker.
- Give the reward when your child reaches their goal. If your child does not reach their goal, do not criticise or take away stickers they have earned.
- When your child is reaching their goal every day, start to phase out rewards by making them harder to achieve. For example, only give a reward every second day, then at the end of the week. If your child is working for a weekly reward, you can make the reward a family event for your child to look forward to. Special events that are not possible to organise daily can provide extra motivation for your child.
- Gradually phase out the chart and make rewards less predictable by giving them every now and then. Continue to praise your child for behaving well. Continue to use consequences if problem behaviour occurs (see Week 3: Managing Misbehaviour).

EXERCISE 10 *Setting up a behaviour chart*

Write down the behaviour for which you plan to use a chart. Make sure you phrase it positively. For example, the target behaviour would be *Doing as you are told* rather than *Not being disobedient* or *Talking nicely* rather than *Not swearing* or *Sharing* rather than *Not fighting over toys*. Make sure the behaviour is clear to your child.

....

....

....

....

Think of what your child can receive for the desired behaviour/s (e.g. stickers, stamps, smiley faces, points, stars), and how many they need to earn to receive a back-up reward. Remember to set easy goals at first so your child is rewarded for their extra effort, then you can gradually make the goals harder to achieve. Ideally your child should earn a back-up reward on the first day of the chart.

....

....

....

....

Describe the back-up rewards that your child can earn for a specified number of stars or stickers. Choose rewards that your child will enjoy, such as having a friend over to play, riding bikes in the park or choosing their favourite dinner. You can discuss this with your child to get their ideas on things they would like to work for.

....

....

....

....

Next week, you will need to decide what consequences you can apply if your child fails to complete the desired behaviour. You will look at consequences in detail next week.

List anything you need to purchase or get organised before you can start using the chart (e.g. stickers, back-up rewards).

....

....

....

....

CONCLUSION

Summary of Activities

In Week 2, ten positive parenting strategies were introduced. These included:

- spending quality time with your child
- talking with your child
- showing affection
- praising your child
- giving your child attention
- providing engaging activities
- setting a good example
- using incidental teaching
- using Ask, Say, Do
- using behaviour charts

■ PRACTICE EXERCISES

- Choose two strategies to try out with your child. Set specific goals such as *I will use descriptive praise five times each day* and *I will use Ask, Say, Do each evening to help my child brush their teeth*. Keep track of how you go by using the monitoring form on page 43. Each day, write 'Y' for Yes or 'N' for No in the column under each goal. A space is provided for writing any comments, reactions or obstacles to reaching your daily goals (e.g. *Ben loved being praised*, or *I just didn't have the energy to spend time with the kids today*). An additional copy of this form is included in the Worksheets section. Jot down the two strategies you plan to use over the next 7 days.

....

....

....

....

- Ask your child what reward they would like to work for on their behaviour chart. You can write these rewards on page 40.
- Get materials together and prepare a behaviour chart but do not start using it with your child until after you have completed Week 3: Managing Misbehaviour which will provide more information on what consequences to use if misbehaviour occurs.
- Continue to keep track of your child's behaviour and plot this data on your behaviour graph. As you start to use the strategies introduced this week, look for changes in your child's behaviour.

■ OPTIONAL HOMEWORK

For a review of the material covered this week, you may like to watch:

- *Every Parent's Survival Guide*, Part 3, Promoting Children's Development

Content of Next Week

Week 3 will look at practical strategies for managing misbehaviour and helping children to develop self-control.

CHECKLIST FOR PROMOTING CHILDREN'S DEVELOPMENT

Choose two of the strategies introduced in Week 2 which you would like to practise with your child over the next week. Be as specific as possible (e.g. one goal may be to use descriptive praise statements with your child at least five times per day). Use the table below to record whether you reached your goals each day. Comment on what went well and list any problems that occurred.

GOAL 1:
....
....

GOAL 2:
....
....

DAY	GOAL 1 Y/N	GOAL 2 Y/N	COMMENTS
1			
2			
3			
4			
5			
6			
7			

Week 2

Managing Misbehaviour

Week 3

OVERVIEW

All children need to learn to accept limits and to control their disappointment when they do not get what they want. Managing these situations can be challenging for parents, but there are positive and effective ways to help children learn self-control. Children learn self-control when their parents use consequences for misbehaviour *immediately*, *consistently* and *decisively*. Several options for managing children's problem behaviour will be presented in this chapter. Consider each as an option you could use with your family. You may find some strategies you would like to use with your child.

OBJECTIVES

By the end of Week 3, you should be able to:

- Set appropriate ground rules and discuss them with your family.
- Use directed discussion and planned ignoring to deal with mild problem behaviour.
- Give clear, calm instructions to your child.
- Back up your instructions with logical consequences, quiet time or time-out.
- Put a behaviour chart into practice.

Week 3

Managing Misbehaviour

A number of strategies for helping children deal with frustration and accept limits are presented in this chapter. You may have heard about and already use some of these strategies and some may be new to you. Use this as a chance to think about your approach to discipline and to fine-tune it. Ask yourself these questions: Do I have a discipline strategy? Do I have a back up if my first line approach doesn't work? How effective is it? Does it teach my child how they are expected to behave? As you look at each strategy think about when the strategy could be used in your family.

It is important to remember that all strategies have their limitations and no single strategy will work for all situations. Sometimes several strategies are needed in combination rather than in isolation. To be effective, the strategies introduced in this chapter must be used in conjunction with the strategies introduced in Week 2.

Establish clear ground rules

Recommended age range: 3–12 years. Children need limits to know what is expected of them and how they should behave. A few basic house rules (four or five) can help. Rules should tell children what to do, rather than what not to do. *Walk in the house, Speak in a pleasant voice* and *Keep your hands and feet to yourself* are better rules than *Don't run, Don't shout* and *Don't fight*. Rules work best when they are fair, easy to follow, and you can back them up. Try to involve your child in deciding on family rules.

You may like to call a family meeting and decide on some rules with your family. The key points to remember are:

- have a small number of rules
- rules should be fair
- rules should be easy to follow
- rules should be enforceable
- rules should be positively stated

EXERCISE **1** *Deciding on ground rules*

In the space provided, list four or five rules that you would like to use in your home.

....

....

....

....

Use directed discussion to deal with rule breaking

Recommended age range: 3–12 years. Directed discussion is best used when a child occasionally forgets a basic house rule. It involves gaining your child's attention, telling your child the problem, explaining briefly why it is a problem and describing or getting your child to suggest the correct behaviour. The correct behaviour can then be practised.

For example, *Carl, you are running in the house, you might break something. What's our rule about moving in the house?… Now you show me the right way to move in the house. Go back to the door and start again.* To make directed discussion even better, get your child to practise the correct behaviour twice. If your child does not follow this instruction, use quiet time (see page 52).

EXERCISE **2** *Ideas for using directed discussion*

Think of a rule that occasionally gets broken in your house or imagine that your child has just broken one of your new rules. Write down what you could say to your child at each step of a directed discussion to teach your child the correct behaviour.

Situation:

....

....

Gain your child's attention.

....

....

State the problem briefly, simply and calmly.

....

....

Week **3**

Briefly explain why the behaviour is a problem.

....

....

Describe or ask your child to suggest the correct behaviour.

....

....

Have your child practise the correct behaviour.

....

....

Praise your child for the correct behaviour.

....

....

Use planned ignoring to deal with minor problem behaviour

Recommended age range: 1–7 years. Planned ignoring means to deliberately pay no attention to a child when a minor problem behaviour occurs. Minor problems include whining, using a silly voice and saying rude words. When you ignore a behaviour, do not look at or talk to your child. Your child may become quite noisy at first, to try to get your attention. If necessary, turn and walk away. Try to stay calm and make sure your body language stays neutral. If needed, take some slow, deep breaths to help you remain calm. Keep ignoring as long as the problem behaviour continues. As soon as your child stops the problem behaviour and behaves appropriately, praise them. Do not ignore more severe problems such as when your child hurts someone or damages property. Take action quickly and decisively (see Exercises 4–7).

For which minor problem behaviours could you use planned ignoring?

....

....

....

....

When do you stop ignoring a minor problem behaviour?

....

....

....

....

What would stop you from using planned ignoring?

....

....

....

....

Week 3

Give clear, calm instructions

Recommended age range: 2–12 years. It is important to give children instructions that are clear and direct. When you want your child to do something, be prepared to back up your instruction. It is not reasonable to always insist on instant obedience. When you want your child to start a new task, where possible, let your child finish what they are doing, or wait for a break in their activity, before giving an instruction. If a problem behaviour is occurring, act immediately. When you want your child to do something, follow these steps:

Get close and gain your child's attention

Stop what you are doing and move to within an arm's length of your child. Bend down to their eye level and use your child's name to gain their attention.

Tell your child what to do

Be specific, say exactly what you want your child to do — *Heidi, it's time for dinner. Come to the table now please.* If you want your child to stop doing something, be sure to tell them what to do instead — *Theo, stop hitting your brother. Keep your hands to yourself.*

Give your child time to cooperate

Pause briefly to give your child time to do what you have asked. Around 5 seconds is enough. Stay close and watch your child.

Praise cooperation

If your child cooperates with your request, praise them — *Max, thank you for doing as I asked.*

Repeat your instruction

If your instruction was to start a new task, such as getting ready for bed, repeat the instruction once if your child does not cooperate within 5 seconds. If you have asked your child to stop doing something, do not repeat the instruction.

Back up your instruction

If your child does not cooperate, back up your request with a consequence (see Exercises 5, 6 and 7).

EXERCISE 4 *Ideas for giving clear, calm instructions*

Write down some examples of clear, calm instructions you could use in the following situations. Indicate how many times you would give the instruction to your child:

It is time for your child's dinner.

....

....

....

Your child is jumping on the couch.

....

....

....

Your child's toys are scattered on the floor.

....

....

....

> Your child is interrupting your telephone call.
>
> ....
>
> ....
>
> ....
>
> It is time for your child to get ready to go out.
>
> ....
>
> ....
>
> ....

Back up your instructions with logical consequences

Recommended age range: 2–12 years. Logical consequences are best used for mild problem behaviours that do not occur too often. If your child does not follow a rule or a clear instruction, then choose a consequence that fits the situation. If possible, remove the activity or the toy that is at the centre of the problem. Logical consequences work best if they are brief — 5 to 30 minutes is usually long enough. When a problem occurs, follow these steps:

Withdraw the activity

Do not debate or argue the point with your child. Act as soon as the problem occurs. Explain why you are removing the toy or activity — *You are not sharing the puzzle, I'm putting it away for 5 minutes*, or *You won't wear your helmet, so you can put your bike away for 30 minutes*, or *You are still arguing over the television, TV is off for 10 minutes*, or *You are not keeping the sand on the ground, you must stay out of the sand pit now for 5 minutes.*

Return the activity

Remember to keep to the agreement. When the time is up, return the activity so that your child can practise how to behave appropriately. Try to prevent the same thing happening again by helping your child solve the problem, such as helping them decide who will have the first turn.

Use another consequence if necessary

If a problem happens again after giving the activity back to your child, follow up by removing the activity for a longer period, such as the rest of the day, or use quiet time (see page 52).

Think of some logical consequences for the following situations and make a note of what you would say to your child.

Your child is playing with their drink at the dinner table.

....

....

....

Your child is playing roughly with a toy.

....

....

....

Your child is wandering away from you on a walk.

....

....

....

Your child is playing dangerously on the swings.

....

....

....

Your child is drawing on the wall.

....

....

....

Use quiet time to deal with misbehaviour

Recommended age range: 18 months–10 years. Quiet time is a brief, mild and effective way of helping children learn more acceptable behaviour. Use quiet time if your child does not do as you have asked. Quiet time involves removing your child from the activity in which a problem has occurred and having them sit quietly on the edge of the activity for a short time. When your child is in quiet time, do not give them any attention. This is a time for them to be quiet, not a time to talk or attract attention. Once your child has remained quiet for the set time, they can rejoin the activity.

Quiet time is usually in the same room in which the problem occurred. A toddler's cot or playpen can be used as a quiet area for children as young as 18 months. Older children can sit on the floor or in a chair. Short periods in quiet time are more effective than longer ones. One minute of quiet for 2-year-olds, 2 minutes for 3 to 5-year-olds and a maximum of 5 minutes can be used for children aged between 5 and 10 years.

It is important that your child knows what to expect before you start using quiet time. Sit down and explain which specific behaviours will earn quiet time and show your child what will happen by walking them through the steps of the quiet time routine. Explain the rules of quiet time. Check that your child understands they need to be quiet for a set time before they can come out of quiet time.

When misbehaviour occurs, follow these steps:

Tell your child what to do

Act quickly when you see a problem behaviour occurring. Get close to your child, gain their attention and tell them what to do — *Daniel, stop pushing your sister now, play gently with her*. If the problem behaviour stops, praise your child for doing as you asked.

Back up your instruction with quiet time

If the problem behaviour continues or occurs again within the next hour, tell your child what they have done wrong — *You have not stopped pushing your sister* — and the consequence — *Now go to quiet time*. Be calm and firm. If necessary, take your child to quiet time. Ignore any protests and do not lecture, argue or nag.

Remind your child of the rules

As you put your child in quiet time, remind them that they can rejoin the activity when they have been quiet for the set time. If your child does not sit quietly in quiet time, take them to time-out (see page 55).

After quiet time

When quiet time is over, do not mention the incident. Encourage your child to find something to do. Praise your child for desirable behaviour as soon as possible after quiet time. If the problem behaviour occurs again, you will need to repeat the quiet time routine.

EXERCISE 6 *Preparing to use quiet time*

What space in your home could be used for quiet time?

....

....

What can you say to your child as you take them to quiet time?

....

....

....

What can you say to your child as you put them in quiet time?

....

....

....

How long will your child need to be quiet in quiet time?

....

....

When can you talk to your child again?

....

....

What can you say to your child when quiet time is over?

....

....

....

What can you do if your child is not quiet within 10 seconds or does not stay seated in quiet time?

....

....

....

....

Use time-out to deal with serious misbehaviour

Recommended age range: 2–10 years. Time-out is a positive strategy to use instead of shouting at, threatening or smacking a child who has misbehaved. When it is used correctly, it can be an extremely effective way of helping children learn self-control and more acceptable behaviour. The main advantage of time-out is that it requires you, the parent, to remain calm. If you become angry, you risk losing your temper and hurting your child. Time-out gives everyone the chance to calm down. You can use time-out when your child does not stay in quiet time, or as a consequence for temper outbursts or serious misbehaviour such as hurting others.

Time-out works in much the same way as quiet time except your child is put in another room away from everyone else. Leave the door open, although you may need to close it if your child does not stay in the room. If your child's bedroom is full of toys and other interesting activities, you might need to consider using another room for time-out. Time-out should be in a room that is uninteresting, yet safe, with good lighting and ventilation. For example, child-proof your bathroom for time-out by removing or locking away anything that might be dangerous.

Short periods in time-out are more effective than longer ones. One minute of quiet for 2-year-olds, 2 minutes for 3 to 5-year-olds and a maximum of 5 minutes can be used for children aged between 5 and 10 years.

It is important that your child knows what to expect before you start using time-out. Sit down and explain what specific behaviours will earn time-out and show your child what will happen by walking them through the steps of the time-out routine. Explain the rules of time-out. Check that your child understands they need to be quiet for a set time before they can come out of time-out.

The guidelines for using time-out are similar to those for quiet time. When serious misbehaviour occurs, follow these steps:

Tell your child what to do

Act quickly when you see a problem behaviour occurring. Get close and gain your child's attention. Tell them what to stop doing — *Dana, stop screaming now* — and what to do instead — *Use your quiet voice.* Praise your child if they do as you ask.

Back up your instruction with time-out

If your child does not stop the misbehaviour within 5 seconds, tell them what they have done wrong — *You have not done as I asked* — and the consequence — *Go to time-out now, please.* Be calm and firm. If necessary, take your child to time-out. Ignore any protests and do not lecture, argue or nag.

Remind your child of the rules

As you put your child in time-out, remind them that they can come out when they have been quiet for the set time. Leave the door open, although you may need to close it if your child does not stay in the room.

Ignore misbehaviour in time-out

Some children may continue to misbehave in time-out, such as kicking, screaming or calling out. If you pay attention to this behaviour, time-out will not work. You must be prepared to persist with this technique. Do not talk to your child or give them any attention until they have been quiet for the set time.

After time-out

When time-out is over, do not talk about the incident again. Encourage your child to get involved in an activity. Watch for your child behaving well and praise them. If the problem behaviour occurs again, you will need to repeat the time-out routine.

Keep track

You may find it helpful to write down each time you use time-out and how long it takes before your child is quiet for the set time (see the *Diary of Time-Out* on page 70). As your child learns the time-out routine, they should become quiet more quickly and time-out should be needed less often. If problems occur when you use time-out or things do not seem to be getting better by the end of the second week, it is important to seek professional help.

Common problems with time-out

Parents who have tried a version of time-out may have found that it has not worked for one of the following reasons:

- *The child has been allowed to decide when to come out.* For example, the parent may say — *Amanda, don't speak like that in this house. Go to your room and come out when you're ready to behave yourself.* The child may simply walk into their room and come straight out again.
- *Time-out has been used inconsistently.* Time-out works best when parents use it every time a problem behaviour occurs, rather than threatening to use it or using it from time to time.
- *The child comes out of time-out while they are still upset.* This is a major problem because the child learns that if they yell loud and long enough they will get out. Getting out of time-out should depend on the child actually being quiet rather than promising to be good or simply being there for a set time. Time-out starts when all noises and protesting stop.

What room or space could you use for time-out in your home?

....

....

What can you say to your child as you take them to time-out?

....

....

....

What can you say to your child as you put them in time-out?

....

....

....

....

How long will your child need to be quiet in time-out?

....

....

When can you talk to your child again?

....

....

What can you say to your child when time-out is over?

....

....

....

....

What could you do if your child refused to come out of time-out when it was over?

....

....

....

....

Week 3

What could you do if your child made a mess in the time-out room?

....

....

....

....

What could you do if your child came out of time-out before their time was up?

....

....

....

....

What could happen if you threaten to use time-out with your child?

....

....

....

....

What could happen if you let your child out of time-out while they are still upset?

....

....

....

....

Common questions about time-out

- *What if my child screams and carries on for ages?* It is important to remember that eventually your child will stop. It may take 15 to 30 minutes or more but your child will stop if they do not get any attention for escalating. To break the escalation trap, children need to learn that getting louder or persisting with their demands will not get your attention. Attention will only come when they have been quiet for the set time in time-out. You may find it helpful to take yourself as far away as possible, but still within hearing distance, such as to the garden with a cup of tea, or telephone someone for support. Time-out will only work if you ignore all screams and other noises such as kicking or banging on the walls. The set time for time-out (2–5 minutes) does not start until your child is quiet.

- *What if my child calls out for something?* Children often try to get some attention from their parents when they are in time-out. They may make all sorts of requests, such as *How much longer Mum?* or *Can I come out now? I'll be good, I promise!* or *I'm thirsty, I need a drink!* If parents respond to these requests, children get social attention which works as an accidental reward for escalating. This can encourage children to call out more next time they go to time-out. To help your child learn to settle quickly in time-out, do not answer these questions. However, if your child asks to go to the toilet, take them matter-of-factly (without talking) to the toilet and return them to time-out as soon as they have finished using the toilet.

- *What if my child says they like going to time-out and they don't care if they have to go?* Use planned ignoring to respond to comments like this. Do not say anything but take your child straight to time-out. If these comments do not get a reaction, your child will stop making them.

- *What if my child runs away when I say time-out?* To avoid this problem, try to get close to your child before giving an instruction. However, if your child does run away, do not chase them as this may turn into a game. Wait until your child comes back within arm's reach, perhaps as much as 15 minutes later. As soon as they are close to you, take them by the hand and go straight to time-out. Since running away does not lead to a reward for your child (as they still need to go to time-out), they will learn not to run away.

- *What if my child promises to be good when I say they have to go to time-out?* The aim is for your child to learn to follow your instructions rather than threats of time-out. To help break the escalation trap and to help your child learn to follow clear, calm instructions, back up our instructions with immediate consequences. Take your child to time-out — do not back down or else your child will learn to promise to be good whenever you say *time-out*.

- *What if I forget my child is in time-out and they call out to say they've been quiet?* Try to keep track of the time your child is quiet in time-out to help your child learn to settle quickly. However, sometimes you may be busy and forget to let your child out of time-out when they have been quiet for the set time. If this happens and your child calls out, do not let them out of time-out straight away. Wait about 30–40 seconds and then let them out. If you let your child out immediately, they may think they need to call out rather than stay quiet to get out of time-out.

- *What if my child makes a mess in time-out?* To help avoid this problem, choose your time-out room carefully. Choose a room in which it is difficult to make a mess. For example, in a child-proof bathroom, a child can only empty the dirty clothes basket or pull the towels off the rack. If your child makes a mess in time-out, wait until your child has been quiet for the set time before going to them. Stay calm and matter-of-fact. Tell your child they have been quiet for the set time and that they can come out when they have tidied the room (i.e. use a logical consequence). Remember to have realistic expectations of how well your child can tidy up given their age.

- *What if my child breaks things in time-out?* Aggressive or destructive behaviour is unlikely to occur for the first time in time-out — it is likely you have seen it before. If your child has been destructive in the past, you will need to set up your time-out area carefully. Make sure you choose a space for time-out where little can be damaged. It is also a good idea to remove your child's shoes before putting your child in time-out. Remember to stay calm and look after yourself when your child is in time-out. For example, listen to some music or telephone a friend. Do not talk to or go to your child unless you feel they are in danger. When your child has been quiet for the set time, let them out of time-out. If your child causes any damage, use a logical consequence such as loss of pocket money or extra chores to help pay for any damage caused. It can be helpful to remind yourself that it is always possible to repair a hole in the wall. However, children who have difficulty managing their anger often become adults who have difficulty managing their anger. If left unchecked, aggressive and destructive behaviour can lead to life-long problems.

Developing Parenting Routines

The flow chart on the next page shows how to put together some of these strategies to create a compliance routine. This routine is useful when you want your child to start doing a new task such as getting ready for bed, bath or dinner. By following this routine you can break the escalation trap referred to in Week 1. It is likely that you will remain calm and your child will have less time to escalate if you follow these steps.

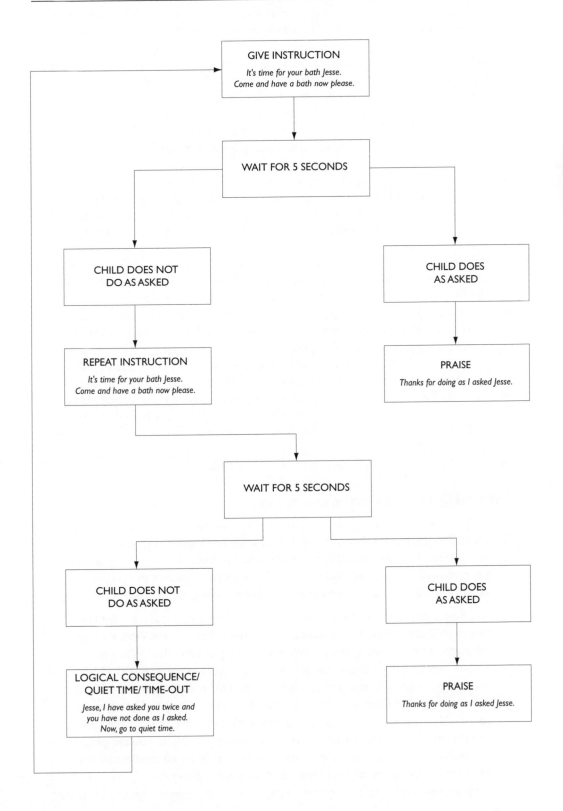

Points to remember

- When giving instructions, make them clear and direct — tell your child exactly what you would like them to do. Avoid asking questions or giving vague statements.
- After you have given your instruction, wait for 5 seconds to give your child time to follow your instruction. Try not to talk to your child — use planned ignoring if your child talks to you during this 5 second period. Do not argue or debate the point — simply stay calm and wait.
- Avoid using general praise comments such as *good boy* or *thanks* when your child does as you asked. Tell your child exactly what they have done that pleases you.
- If you have to repeat your instruction, stay calm and simply repeat the same words. Do not get angry or raise your voice.
- Once you have said your child must go to quiet time, do not argue or debate the point. If your child says they will do as you ask at this point, use planned ignoring. Be consistent and follow through with the consequence. This will help your child learn to follow instructions rather than threats to use logical consequences, quiet time or time-out.
- If your child does not go to quiet time or time-out when you tell them to, guide them by the shoulders until they start to walk there on their own. With small children, you can pick your child up and carry them if necessary.
- When you put your child in quiet time, tell them the quiet time rules — *You need to stay here and be quiet for 2 minutes*. Give this reminder even if your child is upset.
- If your child does not follow the quiet time rules, use time-out as a back-up to quiet time — *Jesse you have not stayed quietly in quiet time. Now you must go to time-out.* Ignore any protesting. If necessary, pick your child up and carry them to time-out.
- After the logical consequence, or after your child has been quiet in quiet time or time-out for the set period, let them out. Then repeat your original instruction — *Thanks for being quiet in quiet time Jesse, you can come out now. OK it's bath time. Go to the bath now please*.
- Repeat this routine until your child does as you ask.

EXERCISE 8 *Using the compliance routine*

Try to practise this routine with another adult before using it with your child. This practise exercise can help you decide whether this is a strategy you would feel comfortable using with your child. It also gives you a chance to practise the words you would actually say to your child before having to do so.

To set up a practice exercise you will need to find another person to play the role of your child or perhaps you could use a teddy bear or doll. Walk through the steps of the routine as though you were talking to your child. When practising, it may be helpful to use the following scene. Let's imagine your child has been playing with their toys and you have warned them at 6:40pm and 6:55pm that they will need to have a bath at 7:00pm. It is now 7:00pm and you give your child a clear instruction to go and have their bath now. The first time you practise this routine, imagine that your child does as you ask, so you can practise praising them. On the next practice, have your child be disobedient so that you need to take them to quiet time and if necessary time-out.

When you want your child to stop a problem behaviour, another routine can be helpful. When a problem is occurring, only give your child one instruction and no reminder (see below). Example routines for managing aggression, tantrums, whining and interrupting are presented on page 64. Notice the similarities across these four routines.

BEHAVIOUR CORRECTION ROUTINE

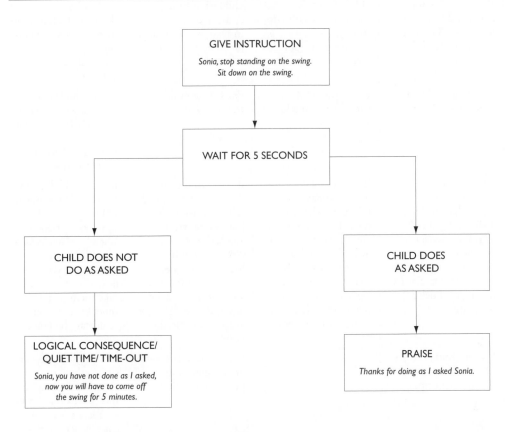

GIVE INSTRUCTION

Sonia, stop standing on the swing.
Sit down on the swing.

WAIT FOR 5 SECONDS

CHILD DOES NOT
DO AS ASKED

CHILD DOES
AS ASKED

LOGICAL CONSEQUENCE/
QUIET TIME/ TIME-OUT

Sonia, you have not done as I asked,
now you will have to come off
the swing for 5 minutes.

PRAISE

Thanks for doing as I asked Sonia.

Week 3

FIGHTING OR REFUSING TO SHARE	TANTRUMS OR TEMPER OUTBURSTS	WHINING OR COMPLAINING	INTERRUPTING
Gain your child's attention. Tell your child what to stop doing and what to do instead — *Stop fighting over the game. Take turns please.*	Gain your child's attention. Tell your child what to stop doing and what to do instead — *Please stop screaming and speak in a nice voice.*	Gain your child's attention. Tell your child what to stop doing and what to do instead — *Stop whining for an icecream. Please ask nicely.*	Gain your child's attention. Tell your child what to stop doing and what to do instead — *Stop interrupting. Say "Excuse-me" and wait until I am free.*
Praise the children if they do as you ask.	Praise your child if they do as you ask.	Praise your child if they do as you ask.	If your child does as you ask, when there is a break in your activity, praise your child for waiting and give them your attention.
If the problem continues, tell your child what they have done wrong and the logical consequence — *You are not sharing the game, I'm putting it away for 5 minutes.* Do not argue or debate the point.	If your child does not do as you have asked, tell them what they have done wrong — *You have not done as I asked* — and the consequence — *Now go to time-out.* Do not argue or debate the point. Take them straight to time-out.	If your child does not do as you have asked, tell them what they have done wrong — *You have not asked nicely* — and the logical consequence — *The icecream goes away for 10 minutes. Try again then.* Do not argue or debate the point.	If your child does not do as you have asked, tell them what they have done wrong — *You are still interrupting* — and the consequence — *Now go to quiet time.* If necessary, take them to quiet time. Do not argue or debate the point.
If your child protests or complains, use planned ignoring.		If your child protests or complains, use planned ignoring.	If your child does not sit quietly in quiet time, tell them what they have done wrong — *You are not being quiet in quiet time* — and the consequence — *Now you must go to time-out.* Take them straight to time-out.
When the time is up, return the activity. Praise the children for sharing and taking turns. If the problem happens again, repeat the consequence for a longer period or use quiet time.	When your child has been quiet for the set time in time-out, set them up in an activity and praise them for behaving well.	When the time is up, if your child has stopped whining, praise them for being quiet and give them an opportunity to ask nicely. If your child asks nicely, praise them and respond to their request. If the problem happens again, repeat the consequence for a longer period or use quiet time.	When your child has been quiet for the set time in quiet time or time-out, set them up in an activity and praise them for behaving well.

EXERCISE 9 *Using the behaviour correction routine*

Choose a problem behaviour and, in the space below, write what you would say or do for each of the main steps involved in stopping this problem using a behaviour correction routine.

Problem Behaviour:

....

....

1. Gain your child's attention. Tell them what to stop doing and what to do instead.

....

....

2. Praise your child if they do as you ask.

....

....

3. If your child does not do as you have asked, tell them the problem and the consequence and enforce the consequence.

....

....

4. Ignore any protests or complaints. Back up your consequence if needed.

....

....

5. When the consequence is over, set your child up in an activity and praise them for behaving well.

....

....

Finalising Your Behaviour Chart

A number of strategies have been introduced for dealing with misbehaviour. Think about the behaviour chart you planned in Week 2. The final step involves determining the consequences for when your child does not reach the set goal and for when they actually misbehave.

EXERCISE 10 *Consequences for behaviour charts*

> What could you do if your child fails to reach the set goal?
>
> ....
>
> ....
>
> ....
>
> ....
>
> What could you do if your child misbehaves (e.g. throws a tantrum)?
>
> ....
>
> ....
>
> ....
>
> ....

CONCLUSION

Summary of Session

In today's session, seven strategies for managing children's misbehaviour were introduced. These included:

- establishing clear ground rules
- using directed discussion to deal with rule breaking
- using planned ignoring to deal with minor problem behaviour
- giving clear, calm instructions
- backing up instructions with logical consequences
- using quiet time to deal with misbehaviour
- using time-out to deal with serious misbehaviour

You were also introduced to the compliance routine and behaviour correction routine which include some of these strategies. You have also had an opportunity to finalise your behaviour chart.

- Decide on four or five ground rules and discuss them with your family.
- Choose the strategies that you would like to try out with your child. If you choose to use quiet time or time-out, keep track of how you go. Use the monitoring form on page 68. An additional copy of this form is provided in the Worksheets section. Choose a time to talk to your child about your new strategies before you use them. If possible, start using your new strategies on a day when you are likely to be at home and when you do not have any time pressures or other tasks that must be completed. Jot down the strategies you plan to use over the next 7 days.

....

....

....

....

- Put into practice the behaviour chart you designed in Week 2, with the consequences you have just decided upon.
- Continue to keep track of your child's behaviour and plot this data on your behaviour graph. As you start to use the strategies introduced this week and in Week 2, look for changes in your child's behaviour.

Week 3

■ OPTIONAL HOMEWORK

For a review of the material covered this week, you may like to watch:

- *Every Parent's Survival Guide,* Part 4, Managing Misbehaviour

Content of Next Week

In Week 4, you will be encouraged to design a structured exercise to practise using some of the positive parenting strategies introduced in Weeks 2 and 3. You will be prompted to track your use of the strategies, identify your strengths and weaknesses and set goals for change.

Week 3

DIARY OF TIME-OUT

Instructions: Make a note of the day, the problem behaviour, when and where it occurred, and the total length of time your child was in time-out.

Set time for time-out: 2 minutes ☐   3 minutes ☐   4 minutes ☐   5 minutes ☐

DAY	PROBLEM BEHAVIOUR	WHEN AND WHERE IT OCCURRED	LENGTH OF TIME-OUT

Using Positive Parenting Strategies 1

OVERVIEW

This week is the first of 3 weeks practice at using the strategies introduced in Weeks 2 and 3. Each week, you will be prompted to choose a time when you can practise using these strategies with your child for about 20 minutes. Aim to set yourself some specific goals for each practice session. You may find it helpful to keep track of your implementation of strategies on the checklists provided. Guidelines for giving yourself some constructive feedback will be introduced. The aim is to identify at least two things you did well during the practice session and one or two things you would do differently. The things you identify as areas for change will become your goals for the rest of the week and for your practice session for Week 5.

OBJECTIVES

By the end of Week 4, you should be able to:
- Use positive parenting strategies effectively with your child.
- Monitor your use of positive parenting strategies.
- Identify your strengths and weaknesses in using positive parenting strategies.
- Set specific goals for further practice.

Getting Started

Schedule a practice session when you will be home with your child. Choose a time when you will be able to spend about 20 minutes in the same room as your child without interruptions from others. Think about some goals you can aim to achieve during the practice session. Aim to use a number of the positive parenting strategies introduced in Weeks 2 and 3. Remember to be as specific as you can when setting goals (e.g. I'll use descriptive praise every 5 minutes and incidental teaching at least twice to encourage independent play; or I'll give four clear, direct instructions and back them up with appropriate consequences when needed — praise for cooperation and logical consequences, quiet time and time-out for disobedience).

For the practice session, turn the television off and do not make any telephone calls. In so doing, you will have more opportunities to interact with your child. If the telephone rings, answer it and try to have a brief conversation. This will give you a chance to use your positive parenting strategies to teach your child to play quietly and wait while you are talking on the telephone. It is also best to stay in the same room or space as your child for the entire practice session. This will allow you to track your child's behaviour and respond to it appropriately.

EXERCISE 1 *Setting up a practice session*

> Identify a time when you will be able to have a 20 minute practice session.
>
> Day .... Date .... Time ....
>
> List your goals for the first practice session.
>
> ....
>
> ....
>
> ....

Designing a Practice Task

Think about how you can structure the practice task to increase the likelihood that you will achieve your goals. For example, if your goal is to use praise and incidental teaching to encourage your child to play independently, you will need to spend part of the practice session with your child and then part of the time doing your own thing. By doing this you will have more opportunities to praise your child for playing by themselves as well as increasing the chance that you will need to use some of the strategies introduced in Week 3 to deal with problem behaviours, such as interrupting and whining. These problem behaviours are more likely to occur when your attention is taken away from your child. If your goal is to give clear, direct instructions, you will need to plan your instructions before the practice session starts. For example, you may spend some time playing with your child and their toys and then ask them to tidy up or wash their hands to change activities or have a snack. This task would give you an opportunity to practise giving instructions and backing them up with consequences. Remember to praise your child for cooperating and use logical consequences, quiet time and time-out for disobedience.

EXERCISE 2 *Planning your practice task*

> Note down how you plan to organise the 20 minutes practice time (e.g. I'll spend 10 minutes with Jack and his toys and then I'll spend 10 minutes ironing clothes and encouraging Jack to continue to play by himself).
>
> ....
>
> ....
>
> ....
>
> ....

Monitoring Your Implementation of Strategies

When you have set your goals and designed your practice task, you are ready to start your practice session. You may find it helpful to set a timer (e.g. on the oven or microwave) to signal the end of the 20 minute session or to prompt you to change activities after 10 minutes.

During the practice task it is a good idea to keep a record of when you are meeting your goals. An example of a completed *Practice Task Checklist* appears on page 72. An additional copy of this form is included in the Worksheets section.

EXERCISE 3 *Keeping track of what you do*

> You may find it helpful to use the *Practice Task Checklist* and the checklists on the following pages to remind yourself of the steps to follow when dealing with some common problem behaviours. You can also refer to them after the practice task to see how well you went. These checklists can help you work out which steps you follow well and any steps you may have forgotten or need to practise. This can help you set goals for change. You can also use the checklists at other times if any of these problem behaviours occur. Extra copies of these checklists are included in the Worksheets section.

Note down your goals for the practice task. Be as specific as possible. Use the table below to record whether you reached your goals. Comment on what went well and list any problems that occurred.

GOAL 1: Give clear, calm instructions and use praise for cooperation with instructions

GOAL 2: If my instructions are ignored, back up with a logical consequence, quiet time or time-out

GOAL 3: Try to use incidental teaching to encourage the children to speak more

	GOAL ACHIEVED? Y/N	COMMENTS
GOAL 1	Y	Instructions were pretty specific. I said "good boy" instead of saying exactly what Phillip was doing well. I forgot to praise sometimes.
GOAL 2	Y	Tried logical consequences and quiet time and said why. Probably repeated instructions too many times before backing up with a consequence.
GOAL 3	N	Most of the time spent dealing with disobedience.

PRACTICE TASK CHECKLIST

Note down your goals for the practice task. Be as specific as possible. Use the table below to record whether you reached your goals. Comment on what went well and list any problems that occurred.

GOAL 1:
....
....

GOAL 2:
....
....

GOAL 3:
....
....

	GOAL ACHIEVED? Y/N	COMMENTS
GOAL 1		
GOAL 2		
GOAL 3		

CHECKLIST FOR MANAGING INTERRUPTING

Instructions: Whenever interrupting parents' conversation or activity occurs, record Yes, No or NA (Not Applicable) for each of the steps below.

Week 4

STEPS TO FOLLOW	DAY				
	STEPS COMPLETED?				
1. Gain your child's attention.					
2. Tell your child what to stop doing and what to do instead — *Stop interrupting. Say "Excuse me" and wait until I am free.*					
3. If your child does as you ask, when there is a break in your activity, praise them for waiting and give them your attention.					
4. If your child does not do as you have asked, tell them what they have done wrong — *You are still interrupting* — and the consequence — *Now go to quiet time.* If necessary, take them to quiet time. Do not argue or debate the point.					
5. If your child does not sit quietly in quiet time, tell them what they have done wrong — *You are not being quiet in quiet time* — and the consequence — *Now you must go to time-out.* Take them straight to time-out.					
6. When your child has been quiet for the set time in quiet time or time-out, set them up in an activity.					
7. As soon as possible, praise your child for behaving well.					
NUMBER OF STEPS COMPLETED CORRECTLY:					

CHECKLIST FOR MANAGING FIGHTING OR NOT SHARING

Instructions: Whenever fighting or not sharing or taking turns with other children occurs, record Yes, No or NA (Not Applicable) for each of the steps below.

STEPS TO FOLLOW	DAY				
	STEPS COMPLETED?				
1. Gain your child's attention.					
2. Tell your child what to stop doing and what to do instead — *Stop pushing in front of each other. Take turns please.*					
3. Praise the children if they do as you ask.					
4. If the problem continues, tell your child what they have done wrong and the logical consequence — *You are not taking turns, I'm putting the game away for 5 minutes.* Do not argue or debate the point.					
5. If your child protests or complains, use planned ignoring.					
6. When the time is up, return the activity.					
7. As soon as possible, praise the children for sharing and taking turns.					
8. If the problem happens again, repeat the logical consequence for a longer period or use quiet time.					
NUMBER OF STEPS COMPLETED CORRECTLY:					

CHECKLIST FOR MANAGING AGGRESSION

Instructions: Whenever aggression occurs, record Yes, No or NA (Not Applicable) for each of the steps below.

STEPS TO FOLLOW	DAY				
	STEPS COMPLETED?				
1. Gain your child's attention.					
2. Tell your child what to stop doing and what to do instead — *Stop kicking. Keep your feet to yourself.*					
3. Praise your child if they do as you ask.					
4. If your child does not do as you have asked, tell them what they have done wrong — *You are still kicking* — and the consequence — *Now go to quiet time.* If necessary, take them to quiet time. Do not argue or debate the point.					
5. If your child does not sit quietly in quiet time, tell them what they have done wrong — *You are not being quiet in quiet time* — and the consequence — *Now you must go to time-out.* Take them straight to time-out.					
6. When your child has been quiet for the set time in quiet time or time-out, set them up in an activity.					
7. As soon as possible, praise your child for behaving well.					
NUMBER OF STEPS COMPLETED CORRECTLY:					

CHECKLIST FOR MANAGING TEMPER OUTBURSTS

Instructions: Whenever temper outbursts (e.g. screaming, crying or stamping feet) occur, record Yes, No or NA (Not Applicable) for each of the steps below.

STEPS TO FOLLOW	DAY				
	STEPS COMPLETED?				
EITHER A) Use planned ignoring for toddlers under 2 years old. **OR** B) Gain your child's attention as best you can and follow the steps below:					
1. Tell your child what to stop doing and what to do instead — *Stop yelling right now. Use a nice voice.*					
2. Praise your child if they do as you ask.					
3. If your child does not do as you have asked, tell them what they have done wrong — *You have not done as I asked* — and the consequence — *Now go to time-out.* Do not argue or debate the point. Take them straight to time-out.					
4. When your child has been quiet for the set time in time-out, set them up in an activity.					
5. As soon as possible, praise your child for behaving well.					
NUMBER OF STEPS COMPLETED CORRECTLY:					

CHECKLIST FOR MANAGING WHINING

Instructions: Whenever whining for something occurs, record Yes, No or NA (Not Applicable) for each of the steps below.

STEPS TO FOLLOW	DAY — STEPS COMPLETED?				
1. Gain your child's attention.					
2. Tell your child what to stop doing and what to do instead — *Stop whining for a piece of cake. Please ask nicely.*					
3. Praise your child if they do as you ask.					
4. If your child does not do as you have asked, tell them what they have done wrong — *You have not asked nicely* — and the logical consequence — *The cake goes away for 10 minutes. Try again then.* Do not argue or debate the point.					
5. If your child protests or complains, use planned ignoring.					
6. When the time is up, if your child has stopped whining, praise them for being quiet and give them an opportunity to ask nicely for what they want.					
7. If your child asks nicely, praise them for asking nicely and respond to their request.					
8. If the problem happens again, repeat the logical consequence for a longer period or use quiet time.					
NUMBER OF STEPS COMPLETED CORRECTLY:					

Week 4

Reviewing Your Performance

Once you have completed your 20 minute practice task, spend some time thinking about what you did well and anything you could do differently next time. Use your completed checklists to help guide you through Exercise 4.

EXERCISE 4 *Reviewing the practice task*

What do you feel *you* did well during the practice task? Aim to identify at least two things you did well (e.g. I used descriptive praise three times, and followed through with the quiet time consequence for misbehaviour). Refer to your goals listed in Exercise 1. Which goals did you achieve?

....

....

....

....

....

....

....

What do you feel *you* could have done differently to improve on this practice task? Be specific and think of one or two things you would do differently if you repeated this practice task (e.g. I need to use more descriptive praise and tell Jack exactly what he has done that pleases me, and I need to stay calm and tell Jack why he is going to quiet time). Think about the goals you set in Exercise 1. Was there a goal that you did not reach?

....

....

....

....

....

....

....

....

4

Week

You may like to use the space below to make notes about any other issues that arose during the practice task.

....

....

....

....

....

....

....

....

CONCLUSION

Summary of Activities

This week, you had a chance to use the positive parenting strategies in a structured practice exercise. You were also able to track your use of the strategies, identify your strengths and weaknesses, and set goals for change.

■ PRACTICE EXERCISES

- Make a note of the skills you would like to practise for the remainder of this week. Be specific and relate your goals to the weaknesses you identified in your practice task (e.g. Stay calm and explain why Jack is going to quiet time, and use more descriptive praise).

....

....

....

....

....

....

....

....

It is a good idea to keep track of your child's behaviour. At this point you need to decide whether to continue monitoring the same behaviour. Use your behaviour graph to aid your decision. Stop monitoring once the behaviour has reached a satisfactory level and has maintained that level for at least five consecutive days. You can then begin monitoring another target behaviour.

For a review of the positive parenting strategies, you may like to watch:

- *Every Parent's Survival Guide,* Part 3, Promoting Children's Development
- *Every Parent's Survival Guide,* Part 4, Managing Misbehaviour

Content of Next Week

Next week you will have another opportunity to track your use of the positive parenting strategies in a structured practice session. You will once again be prompted to identify your strengths and weaknesses and to set goals for change.

Week 4

Using Positive Parenting Strategies 2

5

Week

OVERVIEW

This week gives you another opportunity to practise using the strategies introduced in Weeks 2 and 3. Once again, you will be prompted to choose a 20 minute time period for completing this practice session. The goals for this week's practice session will often be related to the skills you set yourself to practise after your last practice session. Again, you will be prompted to track your performance, identify your strengths and weaknesses and set further goals for change.

OBJECTIVES

By the end of Week 5, you should be able to:

● Use positive parenting strategies effectively with your child.
● Monitor your use of positive parenting strategies.
● Identify your strengths and weaknesses in using positive parenting strategies.
● Set specific goals for further practice.

Getting Started

Schedule a practice session when you will be home with your child. Choose a time when you will be able to spend about 20 minutes in the same room as your child without interruptions from others. Think about some goals you can aim to achieve during the practice session. It may be helpful to refer back to page 80 where you listed skills to practise following your last practice session. Remember to be as specific as you can when setting goals (e.g. I'll use descriptive praise every 5 minutes, I'll stay calm and give four clear, direct instructions and back them up with appropriate consequences when needed — praise for cooperation and logical consequences, quiet time and time-out for disobedience, and if using quiet time, I'll tell Jack why he is going to quiet time).

Remember, for the practice session it is best to turn the television off and not make any telephone calls. In so doing, you will have more opportunities to interact with your child. It is also best to stay in the same room or space as your child for the entire practice session. This will allow you to track your child's behaviour and respond to it appropriately.

EXERCISE 1 *Setting up a practice session*

Identify a time when you will be able to have a 20 minute practice session.

Day .... Date .... Time ....

List your goals for the practice session.

....

....

....

Designing a Practice Task

Think about how you can structure the practice task to increase the likelihood that you will achieve your goals. For example, if you are looking for opportunities to praise your child, it is best if your attention is directed away from your child at least some of the time. In so doing you can praise your child for playing by themselves. If you aim to practise giving instructions, plan your practice session around times when you are more likely to give your child instructions (e.g. when getting ready to go out in the morning you may need to tell your child to get dressed, put their shoes on, brush their hair and teeth and so on). To practise your strategies for dealing with misbehaviour, choose a time of the day or activity that is likely to produce some problem behaviour. Often this simply involves taking your attention away from your child so that you are busy with an activity and your child needs to play independently.

EXERCISE 2 *Planning your practice task*

> Note down how you plan to organise the 20 minutes practice time (e.g. I'll
> start the exercise at 7:00pm when Jack is to start getting ready for bed.
> This will give me a chance to give four or five clear, direct instructions.).
>
> ....
>
> ....
>
> ....
>
> ....

Monitoring Your Implementation of Strategies

When you have set your goals and designed your practice task, you are ready to start
your practice session. You may find it helpful to set a timer (e.g. on the oven or
microwave) to signal the end of the 20 minute session or to prompt you to change
activities after 10 minutes.

EXERCISE 3 *Keeping track of what you do*

> During the practice task try to keep a record of when you are meeting your
> goals. You may find it helpful to use the *Practice Task Checklist* and the checklists
> on the following pages to remind yourself of the steps to follow when dealing
> with some common problem behaviours. You can also refer to them after the
> practice task to see how well you went. These checklists can help you work
> out which steps you follow well and any steps you may have forgotten or
> need to practise. This can help you set goals for change. You can also use the
> checklists at other times if any of these problem behaviours occur. Extra
> copies of these checklists are included in the Worksheets section.

Note down your goals for the practice task. Be as specific as possible. Use the table below to record whether you reached your goals. Comment on what went well and list any problems that occurred.

GOAL 1: ....

....

GOAL 2: ....

....

GOAL 3: ....

....

	GOAL ACHIEVED? Y/N	COMMENTS
GOAL 1		
GOAL 2		
GOAL 3		

CHECKLIST FOR MANAGING INTERRUPTING

Instructions: Whenever interrupting parents' conversation or activity occurs, record Yes, No or NA (Not Applicable) for each of the steps below.

STEPS TO FOLLOW	DAY				
	STEPS COMPLETED?				
1. Gain your child's attention.					
2. Tell your child what to stop doing and what to do instead — *Stop interrupting. Say "Excuse me" and wait until I am free.*					
3. If your child does as you ask, when there is a break in your activity, praise them for waiting and give them your attention.					
4. If your child does not do as you have asked, tell them what they have done wrong — *You are still interrupting* — and the consequence — *Now go to quiet time.* If necessary, take them to quiet time. Do not argue or debate the point.					
5. If your child does not sit quietly in quiet time, tell them what they have done wrong — *You are not being quiet in quiet time* — and the consequence — *Now you must go to time-out.* Take them straight to time-out.					
6. When your child has been quiet for the set time in quiet time or time-out, set them up in an activity.					
7. As soon as possible, praise your child for behaving well.					
NUMBER OF STEPS COMPLETED CORRECTLY:					

Week 5

CHECKLIST FOR MANAGING FIGHTING OR NOT SHARING

Instructions: Whenever fighting or not sharing or taking turns with other children occurs, record Yes, No or NA (Not Applicable) for each of the steps below.

STEPS TO FOLLOW	DAY				
	STEPS COMPLETED?				
1. Gain your child's attention.					
2. Tell your child what to stop doing and what to do instead — *Stop pushing in front of each other. Take turns please.*					
3. Praise the children if they do as you ask.					
4. If the problem continues, tell your child what they have done wrong and the logical consequence — *You are not taking turns, I'm putting the game away for 5 minutes.* Do not argue or debate the point.					
5. If your child protests or complains, use planned ignoring.					
6. When the time is up, return the activity.					
7. As soon as possible, praise the children for sharing and taking turns.					
8. If the problem happens again, repeat the logical consequence for a longer period or use quiet time.					
NUMBER OF STEPS COMPLETED CORRECTLY:					

Week 5

CHECKLIST FOR MANAGING AGGRESSION

Instructions: Whenever aggression occurs, record Yes, No or NA (Not Applicable) for each of the steps below.

STEPS TO FOLLOW	DAY				
	STEPS COMPLETED?				
1. Gain your child's attention.					
2. Tell your child what to stop doing and what to do instead — *Stop kicking. Keep your feet to yourself.*					
3. Praise your child if they do as you ask.					
4. If your child does not do as you have asked, tell them what they have done wrong — *You are still kicking* — and the consequence — *Now go to quiet time.* If necessary, take them to quiet time. Do not argue or debate the point.					
5. If your child does not sit quietly in quiet time, tell them what they have done wrong — *You are not being quiet in quiet time* — and the consequence — *Now you must go to time-out.* Take them straight to time-out.					
6. When your child has been quiet for the set time in quiet time or time-out, set them up in an activity.					
7. As soon as possible, praise your child for behaving well.					
NUMBER OF STEPS COMPLETED CORRECTLY:					

Week 5

CHECKLIST FOR MANAGING TEMPER OUTBURSTS

Instructions: Whenever temper outbursts (e.g. screaming, crying or stamping feet) occur, record Yes, No or NA (Not Applicable) for each of the steps below.

STEPS TO FOLLOW	DAY				
	STEPS COMPLETED?				
EITHER A) Use planned ignoring for toddlers under 2 years old. **OR** B) Gain your child's attention as best you can and follow the steps below:					
1. Tell your child what to stop doing and what to do instead — *Stop yelling right now. Use a nice voice.*					
2. Praise your child if they do as you ask.					
3. If your child does not do as you have asked, tell them what they have done wrong — *You have not done as I asked* — and the consequence — *Now go to time-out.* Do not argue or debate the point. Take them straight to time-out.					
4. When your child has been quiet for the set time in time-out, set them up in an activity.					
5. As soon as possible, praise your child for behaving well.					
NUMBER OF STEPS COMPLETED CORRECTLY:					

CHECKLIST FOR MANAGING WHINING

Instructions: Whenever whining for something occurs, record Yes, No or NA (Not Applicable) for each of the steps below.

STEPS TO FOLLOW	DAY — STEPS COMPLETED?				
1. Gain your child's attention.					
2. Tell your child what to stop doing and what to do instead — *Stop whining for a piece of cake. Please ask nicely.*					
3. Praise your child if they do as you ask.					
4. If your child does not do as you have asked, tell them what they have done wrong — *You have not asked nicely* — and the logical consequence — *The cake goes away for 10 minutes. Try again then.* Do not argue or debate the point.					
5. If your child protests or complains, use planned ignoring.					
6. When the time is up, if your child has stopped whining, praise them for being quiet and give them an opportunity to ask nicely for what they want.					
7. If your child asks nicely, praise them for asking nicely and respond to their request.					
8. If the problem happens again, repeat the logical consequence for a longer period or use quiet time.					
NUMBER OF STEPS COMPLETED CORRECTLY:					

Week 5

Reviewing Your Performance

Once you have completed your 20 minute practice task, spend some time thinking about what you did well and anything you could do differently next time. Use your completed checklists to help guide you through Exercise 4.

EXERCISE 4 *Reviewing the practice task*

What do you feel *you* did well during the practice task? Aim to identify at least two things you did well (e.g. I stayed calmed and gave clear, direct instructions, used descriptive praise when Jack followed instructions and told him why he needed to go to quiet time when he didn't follow instructions). Refer to your goals listed in Exercise 1. Which goals did you achieve?

....

....

....

....

....

....

....

What do you feel *you* could have done differently to improve on this practice task? Be specific and think of one or two things you would do differently if you repeated this practice task (e.g. I need to stop repeating my instructions several times and follow through with a consequence after I have given an instruction two times, and I need to follow through with my plan rather than debating or arguing the point). Think about the goals you set in Exercise 1. Was there a goal that you did not reach?

....

....

....

....

....

....

....

You may like to use the space below to make notes about any other issues that arose during the practice task.

....

....

....

....

....

....

....

CONCLUSION

Summary of Activities

This week, you had another chance to use the positive parenting strategies in a structured practice exercise. You were also able to track your use of the strategies, identify your strengths and weaknesses, and set goals for change.

■ **PRACTICE EXERCISES**

- Make a note of the skills you would like to practise for the remainder of this week. Be specific and relate your goals to the weaknesses you identified in your practice task (e.g. Only give an instruction two times before backing up with a consequence and follow through with consequences rather than arguing or debating the point with Jack).

....

....

....

....

....

....

....

....

■ **OPTIONAL HOMEWORK**

It is a good idea to keep track of your child's behaviour. At this point you need to decide whether to continue monitoring the same behaviour. Use your behaviour graph to aid your decision. Stop monitoring once the behaviour has reached a satisfactory level and has maintained that level for at least five consecutive days. You can then begin monitoring another target behaviour.

For a review of the positive parenting strategies, you may like to watch:

- *Every Parent's Survival Guide,* Part 3, Promoting Children's Development
- *Every Parent's Survival Guide,* Part 4, Managing Misbehaviour

Content of Next Week

Next week you will have another opportunity to track your use of the positive parenting strategies in a structured practice session. You will once again be prompted to identify your strengths and weaknesses and to set goals for change.

Using Positive Parenting Strategies 3

Week 6

OVERVIEW

This is the third and final week of setting up structured exercises to practise the positive parenting strategies. Plan a 20 minute time period for completing this exercise. The goals for this week's practice session will often be related to the skills you set yourself to practise after your last practice session. Again, you will be prompted to track your performance, identify your strengths and weaknesses and set further goals for change. Before moving on to Week 7, it is expected that you will be using logical consequences, quiet time and/or time-out effectively at home. If you feel these consequences are not working after Week 6, continue to design practice sessions or seek professional help.

OBJECTIVES

By the end of Week 6, you should be able to:

- Use positive parenting strategies effectively with your child.
- Monitor your use of positive parenting strategies.
- Identify your strengths and weaknesses in using positive parenting strategies.
- Set specific goals for further practice.

Getting Started

Schedule a practice session when you will be home with your child. Choose a time when you will be able to spend about 20 minutes in the same room as your child without interruptions from others. Think about some goals you can aim to achieve during the practice session. It may be helpful to refer back to page 93 where you listed skills to practise following your last practice session. Remember to be as specific as you can when setting goals (e.g. I'll use descriptive praise when Jack follows instructions, I'll give an instruction no more than two times before backing up with a consequence, and I'll follow through with consequences straight away rather than arguing or debating with Jack).

Remember, for the practice session it is best to turn the television off and not make any telephone calls. In so doing, you will have more opportunities to interact with your child. It is also best to stay in the same room or space as your child for the entire practice session. This will allow you to track your child's behaviour and respond to it appropriately.

EXERCISE 1 *Setting up a practice session*

Identify a time when you will be able to have a 20 minute practice session.

Day .... Date .... Time ....

List your goals for the practice session.

....

....

....

Designing a Practice Task

Think about how you can structure the practice task to increase the likelihood that you will achieve your goals. If you are looking for opportunities to praise your child, it is best if your attention is directed away from your child at least some of the time. In so doing you can praise your child for playing by themselves. If you aim to practise giving instructions, plan your practice session around times when you are more likely to give your child instructions. When practising your strategies for dealing with misbehaviour, choose a time of the day or activity that is likely to produce some problem behaviour. Often this simply involves taking your attention away from your child so that you are busy with an activity and your child needs to play independently.

EXERCISE 2 *Planning your practice task*

Note down how you plan to organise the 20 minutes practice time (e.g. Between 5:00pm and 5:30pm is a good time as the children have difficulty playing nicely with one another and keeping themselves entertained in this late afternoon period. I will be busy preparing dinner and the children will also need to do their chores).

....

....

....

....

Monitoring Your Implementation of Strategies

When you have set your goals and designed your practice task, you are ready to start your practice session. You may find it helpful to set a timer (e.g. on the oven or microwave) to signal the end of the 20 minute session or to prompt you to change activities after 10 minutes.

EXERCISE 3 *Keeping track of what you do*

During the practice task try to keep a record of when you are meeting your goals. You may find it helpful to use the *Practice Task Checklist* and the checklists on the following pages to remind yourself of the steps to follow when dealing with some common problem behaviours. You can also refer to them after the practice task to see how well you went. These checklists can help you work out which steps you follow well and any steps you may have forgotten or need to practise. This can help you set goals for change. You can also use the checklists at other times if any of these problem behaviours occur. Extra copies of these checklists are included in the Worksheets section.

PRACTICE TASK CHECKLIST

Note down your goals for the practice task. Be as specific as possible. Use the table below to record whether you reached your goals. Comment on what went well and list any problems that occurred.

GOAL 1: ....
....

GOAL 2: ....
....

GOAL 3: ....
....

	GOAL ACHIEVED? Y/N	COMMENTS
GOAL 1		
GOAL 2		
GOAL 3		

Week 6

CHECKLIST FOR MANAGING INTERRUPTING

Instructions: Whenever interrupting parents' conversation or activity occurs, record Yes, No or NA (Not Applicable) for each of the steps below.

STEPS TO FOLLOW	DAY — STEPS COMPLETED?				
1. Gain your child's attention.					
2. Tell your child what to stop doing and what to do instead — *Stop interrupting. Say "Excuse me" and wait until I am free.*					
3. If your child does as you ask, when there is a break in your activity, praise them for waiting and give them your attention.					
4. If your child does not do as you have asked, tell them what they have done wrong — *You are still interrupting* — and the consequence — *Now go to quiet time.* If necessary, take them to quiet time. Do not argue or debate the point.					
5. If your child does not sit quietly in quiet time, tell them what they have done wrong — *You are not being quiet in quiet time* — and the consequence — *Now you must go to time-out.* Take them straight to time-out.					
6. When your child has been quiet for the set time in quiet time or time-out, set them up in an activity.					
7. As soon as possible, praise your child for behaving well.					
NUMBER OF STEPS COMPLETED CORRECTLY:					

6

Week

CHECKLIST FOR MANAGING FIGHTING OR NOT SHARING

Instructions: Whenever fighting or not sharing or taking turns with other children occurs, record Yes, No or NA (Not Applicable) for each of the steps below.

STEPS TO FOLLOW	DAY				
	STEPS COMPLETED?				
1. Gain your child's attention.					
2. Tell your child what to stop doing and what to do instead — *Stop pushing in front of each other. Take turns please.*					
3. Praise the children if they do as you ask.					
4. If the problem continues, tell your child what they have done wrong and the logical consequence — *You are not taking turns, I'm putting the game away for 5 minutes.* Do not argue or debate the point.					
5. If your child protests or complains, use planned ignoring.					
6. When the time is up, return the activity.					
7. As soon as possible, praise the children for sharing and taking turns.					
8. If the problem happens again, repeat the logical consequence for a longer period or use quiet time.					
NUMBER OF STEPS COMPLETED CORRECTLY:					

CHECKLIST FOR MANAGING AGGRESSION

Instructions: Whenever aggression occurs, record Yes, No or NA (Not Applicable) for each of the steps below.

STEPS TO FOLLOW	DAY				
	STEPS COMPLETED?				
1. Gain your child's attention.					
2. Tell your child what to stop doing and what to do instead — *Stop kicking. Keep your feet to yourself.*					
3. Praise your child if they do as you ask.					
4. If your child does not do as you have asked, tell them what they have done wrong — *You are still kicking* — and the consequence — *Now go to quiet time.* If necessary, take them to quiet time. Do not argue or debate the point.					
5. If your child does not sit quietly in quiet time, tell them what they have done wrong — *You are not being quiet in quiet time* — and the consequence — *Now you must go to time-out.* Take them straight to time-out.					
6. When your child has been quiet for the set time in quiet time or time-out, set them up in an activity.					
7. As soon as possible, praise your child for behaving well.					
NUMBER OF STEPS COMPLETED CORRECTLY:					

6

Week

CHECKLIST FOR MANAGING TEMPER OUTBURSTS

Instructions: Whenever temper outbursts (e.g. screaming, crying or stamping feet) occur, record Yes, No or NA (Not Applicable) for each of the steps below.

	DAY					
STEPS TO FOLLOW	STEPS COMPLETED?					
EITHER A) Use planned ignoring for toddlers under 2 years old. **OR** B) Gain your child's attention as best you can and follow the steps below:						
1. Tell your child what to stop doing and what to do instead — *Stop yelling right now. Use a nice voice.*						
2. Praise your child if they do as you ask.						
3. If your child does not do as you have asked, tell them what they have done wrong — *You have not done as I asked* — and the consequence — *Now go to time-out.* Do not argue or debate the point. Take them straight to time-out.						
4. When your child has been quiet for the set time in time-out, set them up in an activity.						
5. As soon as possible, praise your child for behaving well.						
NUMBER OF STEPS COMPLETED CORRECTLY:						

Week 6

CHECKLIST FOR MANAGING WHINING

Instructions: Whenever whining for something occurs, record Yes, No or NA (Not Applicable) for each of the steps below.

STEPS TO FOLLOW	DAY				
	STEPS COMPLETED?				
1. Gain your child's attention.					
2. Tell your child what to stop doing and what to do instead — *Stop whining for a piece of cake. Please ask nicely.*					
3. Praise your child if they do as you ask.					
4. If your child does not do as you have asked, tell them what they have done wrong — *You have not asked nicely* — and the logical consequence — *The cake goes away for 10 minutes. Try again then.* Do not argue or debate the point.					
5. If your child protests or complains, use planned ignoring.					
6. When the time is up, if your child has stopped whining, praise them for being quiet and give them an opportunity to ask nicely for what they want.					
7. If your child asks nicely, praise them for asking nicely and respond to their request.					
8. If the problem happens again, repeat the logical consequence for a longer period or use quiet time.					
NUMBER OF STEPS COMPLETED CORRECTLY:					

Week 6

Reviewing Your Performance

Once you have completed your 20 minute practice task, spend some time thinking about what you did well and anything you could do differently next time. Use your completed checklists to help guide you through Exercise 4.

EXERCISE 4 *Reviewing the practice task*

What do you feel *you* did well during the practice task? Aim to identify at least two things you did well (e.g. I stayed calm and gave clear, direct instructions, I used descriptive praise when Jack and Harry cooperated with instructions, and I only gave an instruction twice before backing it up with the consequence). Refer to your goals listed in Exercise 1. Which goals did you achieve?

....

....

....

....

....

....

....

What do you feel *you* could have done differently to improve on this practice task? Be specific and think of one or two things you would do differently if you repeated this practice task (e.g. I need to work on the timing of my instructions so that the boys have finished their activity or chore before I give an instruction). Think about the goals you set in Exercise 1. Was there a goal that you did not reach?

....

....

....

....

....

....

....

....

You may like to use the space below to make notes about any other issues that arose during the practice task.

....
....
....
....
....
....
....
....

Summary of Activities

This week, you had another chance to use the positive parenting strategies in a structured practice exercise. You were also able to track your use of the strategies, identify your strengths and weaknesses, and set goals for change.

6
Week

■ PRACTICE EXERCISES

- Make a note of the skills you would like to practise for the remainder of this week. Be specific and relate your goals to the weaknesses you identified in your practice task (e.g. Wait until the children have finished their activity before giving them an instruction).

....
....
....
....
....
....
....
....

It is a good idea to keep track of your child's behaviour. At this point you need to decide whether to continue monitoring the same behaviour. Use your behaviour graph to aid your decision. Stop monitoring once the behaviour has reached a satisfactory level and has maintained that level for at least five consecutive days. You can then begin monitoring another target behaviour.

For a review of the positive parenting strategies, you may like to watch:

- *Every Parent's Survival Guide,* Part 3, Promoting Children's Development
- *Every Parent's Survival Guide,* Part 4, Managing Misbehaviour

Content of Next Week

Week 7 will look at family survival tips to help make the task of parenting easier. You will also be introduced to a strategy called Planned Activities for dealing with 'high-risk situations' in which children's behaviour can be particularly difficult to manage.

Week 6

Planning Ahead

OVERVIEW

At this point, you may find that much of your child's behaviour is improving. However, there are often particular times or places, called 'high-risk situations' when managing your child's behaviour can be more difficult. These situations usually occur when the situation is not designed for children (i.e. few activities or play materials are available) and children have little to do. Other high-risk times are when parents have to do too many things at once, or when there is pressure due to time constraints (e.g. the early morning rush to get ready for school and work). Some common high-risk situations include going shopping, visiting friends or relatives, waiting in a queue (e.g. at the bank), and getting ready to go out. In these situations, a little planning ahead is essential. This week you will look at family survival tips and how to apply planned activities routines to your own high-risk situations.

OBJECTIVES

By the end of Week 7, you should be able to:

- Use the family survival tips to help make the task of parenting easier.
- Identify high-risk situations at home and in the community when your child is more likely to be difficult to manage.
- Describe the six steps involved in designing a planned activities routine (i.e. prepare in advance, talk about rules, select engaging activities, encourage appropriate behaviour, use consequences for misbehaviour, and hold a follow-up discussion).
- Design, use and monitor your own planned activities routines for two high-risk situations.

Family Survival Tips

A lot of information has been presented so far in the program about strategies for managing children's behaviour. However, it is easier to look after your child's needs if you also look after your own. Here are some more ideas that can help make parenting easier.

Work as a team

Parenting is easier when both parents (where applicable) and other carers agree on methods of discipline. Parents should support and back up each other's parenting efforts. Before you use new strategies, discuss the plan with your partner and anyone else in a caring role with your child.

Avoid arguments in front of your child

Children are very sensitive to adult conflict. They become distressed if arguments occur often and are not resolved. If you have a major disagreement, try to discuss it at a time when your child is not present.

Get support

Everyone needs support in raising children. Partners, family, friends and neighbours can be good supports. Talk about your ideas and compare experiences.

Have a break

Everyone needs some time away from their children. This is normal and healthy. If your child is being well cared for and you have plenty of quality time together, it will not harm your child if you have a break from them now and then. It is the quality of time spent together that is important, not the amount of time.

EXERCISE 1 *Taking care of yourself*

Who do you rely on for support?

Family ....

Friends ....

Think about one person you could talk to or telephone at least once a week.

....

Week 7

Make a note of things you like to do (on your own or with your partner or friends).

....

....

....

Think about when you can have a break over the next week and who you can call on for child minding.

....

....

High-Risk Situations

A high-risk situation is one in which you still find your child's behaviour challenging or when you feel less in control. Some parents experience difficulties using positive parenting strategies in situations where there are competing demands for their time and attention, when they are in a hurry, when their parenting is under scrutiny from others (e.g. while shopping or visiting), where they do not have ready access to usual consequences, such as a time-out room, and in environments where there is little for children to do. These situations create a special challenge for parents.

EXERCISE 2 *Identifying high-risk parenting situations*

Think of situations which are high-risk for you. Place a tick next to those home and community situations listed below that can be high-risk times for your family. There is space at the bottom for you to add in additional high-risk situations. Rate how confident you are that you can deal with your child's behaviour in each situation. Rate your confidence from 1 (not at all confident) to 10 (extremely confident).

HOME SITUATIONS	✔	RATING
• waking, getting out of bed	☐	☐
• getting dressed	☐	☐
• eating breakfast, lunch or dinner	☐	☐
• using the bathroom or toilet	☐	☐
• when you are busy doing chores	☐	☐
• getting ready to go out (e.g. to school)	☐	☐
• when visitors arrive	☐	☐
• playing indoors or outdoors	☐	☐
• watching television	☐	☐
• when you are on the telephone	☐	☐
• while you are preparing meals	☐	☐
• when siblings come home from school	☐	☐
• when a parent comes home from work	☐	☐
• undressing/getting ready for bed	☐	☐
• bedtime	☐	☐
•	☐	☐
•	☐	☐
•	☐	☐

COMMUNITY SITUATIONS		
• visiting friends or relatives	☐	☐
• going on family outings (e.g. beach)	☐	☐
• birthday/Christmas parties	☐	☐
• weddings/ceremonies/funerals	☐	☐
• annual holidays	☐	☐
• dinner engagements	☐	☐
• visiting the doctor/dentist	☐	☐

Week 1

	✔	RATING
• travelling in the car	☐	☐
• travelling on public transport	☐	☐
• shopping at the supermarket	☐	☐
• going to local shops	☐	☐
• going to the bank	☐	☐
• leaving your child at a daycare/school	☐	☐
• leaving your child with baby-sitters (or other carers)	☐	☐
•	☐	☐
•	☐	☐
•	☐	☐

Planned Activities Routines

Planning ahead for your high-risk situations can avoid many problems. The planned activities strategy involves problem solving ahead of time to prevent behaviour problems from occurring. The main idea is to plan interesting and engaging activities for your child in situations where they might otherwise be bored and disruptive. By being clear about what you would like your child to do, you can help prevent problems from occurring.

At first you may like to set up some practice sessions. Choose a time to try out the new routine in your high-risk situation and show your child how it works. Make sure you are not under any pressure to do particular tasks by a set time. Think about when you could set up a practice session, where it should take place and who should be there. Set easy goals at first and work up to more difficult situations (e.g. start by visiting a friend for 10 minutes then build up to longer visits).

The following steps will form the basis of your plan for dealing with high-risk situations.

Prepare in advance

Identify any advance planning or preparation you could do before you enter the high-risk situation. Have everything ready that you will need for the situation (e.g. have several activities ready, draw up a behaviour chart, have stickers and back-up rewards ready, pack bags and prepare lunches the night before to avoid last minute rushing). For outings, plan your trip to avoid disrupting your child's routine, such as usual mealtimes and sleep times.

Talk about rules

Prepare your child in advance by describing what is going to happen. Decide on rules for appropriate behaviour in the situation and discuss the rules in a relaxed way with your child (e.g. rules for travelling in the car may include: keep your seat-belt on; use a quiet voice; keep your hands and feet to yourself). Ask your child to repeat the rules, giving praise and prompts where necessary. Just prior to entering the high-risk situation, remind your child of the rules.

Select engaging activities

Keep your child interested and engaged in activities in the high-risk situation. Make a list of activities you can use to keep your child entertained. Encourage your child to select some activities of their own. You may need to help them get started. Try to make use of naturally occurring opportunities for fun interactions such as incidental teaching to keep your child interested and to extend their activity (e.g. talk to your child and ask them questions, count things you can see, play games like "I spy").

Use rewards for appropriate behaviour

List rewards your child can receive for following the rules. Make sure the rewards are practical and immediate. You may find it useful to prepare a special behaviour chart for certain high-risk situations. Explain the rewards to your child when you explain the rules. Ask if your child has any other ideas for rewards or any questions, and praise their involvement in this advance planning. Praise your child often for appropriate behaviour in the high-risk situation and give the back-up reward if the rules are followed (e.g. stopping off at the park on the way home).

Use consequences for misbehaviour

List the consequences your child can expect for failing to follow the rules. Explain these consequences to your child when you explain the rules. Make sure the consequences are practical and immediate (e.g. quiet time at the shops may involve having your child sit quietly at the front of the store or in an aisle, and if the difficult behaviour escalates, you may need to seat your child outside the shops or in the car while you wait beside them).

Hold a follow-up discussion

After a high-risk situation, review how things went with your child. Praise your child for following the rules, and if necessary, describe one rule your child forgot to follow. Discuss anything either you or your child feel needs to be changed, and set a goal for the next time the same high-risk situation occurs (e.g. *You did really well staying close to me while we were at the bank today, but next time let's see if you can remember to use your quiet voice in the bank*).

A sample routine for grocery shopping at the supermarket is presented on page 113. This routine shows how all the steps fit together to make a planned activities routine.

IDENTIFY THE HIGH-RISK SITUATION

- Grocery shopping at the supermarket

SPECIFY DETAILS FOR A PRACTICE SESSION (WHEN, WHERE, WHO SHOULD BE PRESENT)

- A brief trip to get bread, milk and juice at the local supermarket
- Mum and one child to be present

LIST ANY ADVANCED PLANNING OR PREPARATION

- Avoid disrupting sleep and mealtimes
- Pack a small snack and drink
- Prepare a shopping list

DECIDE ON RULES

- Stay close to the trolley
- Only touch things when Mum or Dad say to
- Walk down the aisles

SELECT ENGAGING ACTIVITIES

- Having their own shopping list
- Finding products in each aisle
- Putting things in the trolley
- Talking about colours, prices, shapes, sizes, count aisles
- Holding my shopping list, keys or wallet

LIST REWARDS FOR APPROPRIATE BEHAVIOUR

- Praise
- Pushing the trolley
- Special activity with a parent (e.g. trip to the park)
- Food treats or rides
- Tokens to exchange at the end of the shopping trip

LIST CONSEQUENCES FOR MISBEHAVIOUR

- Clear, direct instruction to *Stop* the problem behaviour and what to do instead
- Quiet time in the aisle, mall or car park
- No reward

NOTE ANY GOALS FROM THE FOLLOW-UP DISCUSSION

- Stay close to the trolley

EXERCISE 3 *Developing a planned activities routine*

> Now you have the chance to design your own planned activities routine.
> There is a blank sheet on page 114. Work through one of the high-risk
> situations you indicated on the checklist on pages 110–111.

Identify the high-risk situation

....

Specify details for a practice session (when, where, who should be present)

....

....

....

....

List any advance planning or preparation

....

....

....

Decide on rules

....

....

....

Select engaging activities

....

....

....

List rewards for appropriate behaviour

....

....

....

List consequences for misbehaviour

....

....

....

Note any goals from the follow-up discussion

....

....

....

Week 1

Summary of Activities

This week, family survival tips were introduced to help make the task of parenting easier. In addition, six steps for planning a parenting routine for a high-risk situation were presented:

- preparing in advance
- talking about rules
- selecting engaging activities
- encouraging appropriate behaviour
- using consequences for misbehaviour
- holding a follow-up discussion

■ PRACTICE EXERCISES

- Choose two of your own high-risk situations and develop planned activities routines for each of them. Try out your routine for each situation at least once in the coming week. There are two blank *Planned Activities Routine* forms on pages 117 and 118 and two monitoring forms on pages 119 and 120. To complete these forms, write down the steps of your routine and then note whether or not you completed it in the high-risk situation. Additional copies of these forms are in the Worksheets section. Write down the two high-risk situations you plan to practise this week.

....

....

....

....

Week 1

It is a good idea to keep track of your child's behaviour. At this point you need to decide whether to continue monitoring the same behaviour. Use your behaviour graph to aid your decision. Stop monitoring once the behaviour has reached a satisfactory level and has maintained that level for at least five consecutive days. You can then begin monitoring another target behaviour.

If available, you may like to watch sections of the following videos that are relevant to your family:

- *Every Parent's Guide to Infants and Toddlers*
- *Every Parent's Guide to Preschoolers*
- *Every Parent's Guide to Primary Schoolers*
- or one of the other videos from the *Triple P Video Series*

Content of Next Week

Weeks 8 and 9 are designed to help you continue to put into practice planned activities routines introduced this week. You will be encouraged to continue to design and implement planned activities routines for high-risk situations, evaluate the success of your routines and refine them as necessary.

Week 7

PLANNED ACTIVITIES ROUTINE

Identify the high-risk situation

....

Specify details for a practice session (when, where, who should be present)

....

....

....

....

List any advance planning or preparation

....

....

....

Decide on rules

....

....

....

Select engaging activities

....

....

....

List rewards for appropriate behaviour

....

....

....

List consequences for misbehaviour

....

....

....

Note any goals from the follow-up discussion

....

....

....

Week **7**

PLANNED ACTIVITIES ROUTINE

Identify the high-risk situation

....

Specify details for a practice session (when, where, who should be present)

....

....

....

List any advance planning or preparation

....

....

....

Decide on rules

....

....

....

Select engaging activities

....

....

....

List rewards for appropriate behaviour

....

....

....

List consequences for misbehaviour

....

....

....

Note any goals from the follow-up discussion

....

....

....

Week 1

PLANNED ACTIVITIES CHECKLIST

Situation: _____

Instructions: Whenever this situation occurs record Yes, No or NA (Not Applicable) for
each of the steps below.

STEPS TO FOLLOW	DAY				
	STEPS COMPLETED?				
1					
2					
3					
4					
5					
6					
NUMBER OF STEPS COMPLETED CORRECTLY:					

Week 1

PLANNED ACTIVITIES CHECKLIST

Situation: _____

Instructions: Whenever this situation occurs record Yes, No or NA (Not Applicable) for each of the steps below.

STEPS TO FOLLOW	DAY				
	STEPS COMPLETED?				
1					
2					
3					
4					
5					
6					
NUMBER OF STEPS COMPLETED CORRECTLY:					

Week 1

Implementing Planned Activities Routines I

OVERVIEW

The next two weeks are designed to help you continue to put into practice the strategies introduced last week. Your main tasks this week are to review how successful your planned activities routines have been, refine them as necessary, and continue to design more routines for high-risk situations.

OBJECTIVES

By the end of week 8, you should be able to:

- Set goals and practice tasks to help you meet your goals.
- Plan, use and monitor planned activities routines for high-risk situations as required.
- Access information on parenting issues, if needed.
- Get support from family or friends when needed.

Review of Planned Activities Routines

EXERCISE 1 *Reviewing your use of planned activities routines*

What were your practice exercises from last week?

....

....

....

....

What worked? Please be specific and think of at least two positive points.
It may be helpful to look at your *Planned Activities Checklist/s*.

....

....

....

....

Is there anything that you could have done differently? You may notice some
steps on your *Planned Activities Checklist/s* that you missed or could improve.

....

....

....

....

Further Planning

EXERCISE 2 *Developing more planned activities routines*

Design another one or two planned activities routines for high-risk situations
you indicated on the checklist on pages 110–111. Blank forms are provided on
pages 123 and 124.

Week 8

Identify the high-risk situation

....

Specify details for a practice session (when, where, who should be present)

....

....

....

List any advance planning or preparation

....

....

....

Decide on rules

....

....

....

Select engaging activities

....

....

....

List rewards for appropriate behaviour

....

....

....

List consequences for misbehaviour

....

....

....

Note any goals from the follow-up discussion

....

....

....

Week 8

Identify the high-risk situation

....

Specify details for a practice session (when, where, who should be present)

....

....

....

....

List any advance planning or preparation

....

....

....

Decide on rules

....

....

....

Select engaging activities

....

....

....

List rewards for appropriate behaviour

....

....

....

List consequences for misbehaviour

....

....

....

Note any goals from the follow-up discussion

....

....

....

Week 8

Summary of Activities

List the main points that came up this week that require follow up by you.

....

....

....

■ PRACTICE EXERCISES

- Try out the planned activities routine/s you have just developed at least once in the coming week. There are two blank *Planned Activities Checklists* on pages 126 and 127. An additional copy of this form is included in the Worksheets section.

■ OPTIONAL HOMEWORK

It is a good idea to keep track of your child's behaviour. At this point you need to decide whether to continue monitoring the same behaviour. Use your behaviour graph to aid your decision. Stop monitoring once the behaviour has reached a satisfactory level and has maintained that level for at least five consecutive days. You can then begin monitoring another target behaviour.

If available, you may like to watch sections of the following videos that are relevant to your family:

- *Every Parent's Guide to Infants and Toddlers*
- *Every Parent's Guide to Preschoolers*
- *Every Parent's Guide to Primary Schoolers*
- or one of the other videos from the *Triple P Video Series*

Week 8

Content of Next Week

Week 9 gives you another opportunity to design and implement planned activities routines for high-risk situations, evaluate the success of your routines and refine them as necessary.

PLANNED ACTIVITIES CHECKLIST

Situation: _____

Instructions: Whenever this situation occurs record Yes, No or NA (Not Applicable) for each of the steps below.

STEPS TO FOLLOW	DAY				
	STEPS COMPLETED?				
1					
2					
3					
4					
5					
6					
NUMBER OF STEPS COMPLETED CORRECTLY:					

Week 8

PLANNED ACTIVITIES CHECKLIST

Situation: _____

Instructions: Whenever this situation occurs record Yes, No or NA (Not Applicable) for each of the steps below.

STEPS TO FOLLOW	DAY				
	STEPS COMPLETED?				
1					
2					
3					
4					
5					
6					
NUMBER OF STEPS COMPLETED CORRECTLY:					

Week 8

Implementing Planned Activities Routines 2

Week 9

OVERVIEW

This week is designed to help you continue to put into practice your planned activities routines. You will review how successful your planned activities routines have been, refine them as necessary, and continue to design more routines for high-risk situations.

OBJECTIVES

By the end of Week 9, you should be able to:

- Set goals and practice tasks to help you meet your goals.
- Plan, use and monitor planned activities routines for high-risk situations as required.
- Access information on parenting issues, if needed.
- Get support from family or friends when needed.

Review of Planned Activities Routines

EXERCISE 1 *Reviewing your use of planned activities routines*

What were your practice exercises from last week?

....

....

....

....

What worked? Please be specific and think of at least two positive points. It may be helpful to look at your *Planned Activities Checklist/s.*

....

....

....

....

Is there anything that you could have done differently? You may notice some steps on your *Planned Activities Checklist/s* that you missed or could improve.

....

....

....

....

Further Planning

EXERCISE 2 *Developing more planned activities routines*

Design another one or two planned activities routines for high-risk situations. You may find it helpful to look back at the checklist on pages 110–111. Blank forms are provided on pages 131 and 132.

Week 9

Identify the high-risk situation

....

Specify details for a practice session (when, where, who should be present)

....

....

....

List any advance planning or preparation

....

....

....

Decide on rules

....

....

....

Select engaging activities

....

....

....

List rewards for appropriate behaviour

....

....

....

List consequences for misbehaviour

....

....

....

Note any goals from the follow-up discussion

....

....

....

Week 9

Identify the high-risk situation

....

Specify details for a practice session (when, where, who should be present)

....

....

....

List any advance planning or preparation

....

....

....

Decide on rules

....

....

....

Select engaging activities

....

....

....

List rewards for appropriate behaviour

....

....

....

List consequences for misbehaviour

....

....

....

Note any goals from the follow-up discussion

....

....

....

Week 9

Summary of Activities

List the main points that came up this week that require follow up by you.

....

....

....

■ PRACTICE EXERCISES

- Try out the planned activities routine/s you have just developed at least once in the coming week. There are two blank *Planned Activities Checklists* on pages 134 and 135. An additional copy of this form is included in the Worksheets section.

■ OPTIONAL HOMEWORK

It is a good idea to keep track of your child's behaviour. At this point you need to decide whether to continue monitoring the same behaviour. Use your behaviour graph to aid your decision. Stop monitoring once the behaviour has reached a satisfactory level and has maintained that level for at least five consecutive days. You can then begin monitoring another target behaviour.

If available, you may like to watch sections of the following videos that are relevant to your family:

- *Every Parent's Guide to Infants and Toddlers*
- *Every Parent's Guide to Preschoolers*
- *Every Parent's Guide to Primary Schoolers*
- or one of the other videos from the *Triple P Video Series*

Content of Next Week

Next week you will look at what has changed since you started Self-Help Triple P and whether you have reached the goals you set at the beginning of the program. You will also be encouraged to think about how to keep things going after you have finished Triple P.

Week 9

PLANNED ACTIVITIES CHECKLIST

Situation: _____

Instructions: Whenever this situation occurs record Yes, No or NA (Not Applicable) for each of the steps below.

STEPS TO FOLLOW	DAY				
	STEPS COMPLETED?				
1					
2					
3					
4					
5					
6					
NUMBER OF STEPS COMPLETED CORRECTLY:					

Week 9

PLANNED ACTIVITIES CHECKLIST

Situation: _____

Instructions: Whenever this situation occurs record Yes, No or NA (Not Applicable) for each of the steps below.

STEPS TO FOLLOW	DAY				
	STEPS COMPLETED?				
1					
2					
3					
4					
5					
6					
NUMBER OF STEPS COMPLETED CORRECTLY:					

Week 9

Program Close

Week 10

OVERVIEW

This is the last week of Self-Help Triple P. You will review your progress through the program and look at how to phase out the program and maintain all the changes you have made. You will also think about goals for the future and how to achieve these goals.

OBJECTIVES

By the end of Week 10, you should be able to:

- Plan, use and monitor planned activities routines for high-risk situations as required.
- Access information on parenting issues, if needed.
- Get support from family or friends when needed.
- Solve any parenting problems as they arise.
- Identify changes in your child's and your own behaviour since commencing Self-Help Triple P.
- Maintain the changes you have made so far.
- Set further goals for change in both your child's and your own behaviour and decide how to achieve these goals.

Review of Planned Activities Routines

EXERCISE 1 *Reviewing your use of planned activities routines*

What were your practice exercises from last week?

....

....

....

....

What worked? Please be specific and think of at least two positive points. It may be helpful to look at your *Planned Activities Checklist/s.*

....

....

....

....

Is there anything that you could have done differently? You may notice some steps on your *Planned Activities Checklist/s* that you missed or could improve.

....

....

....

....

Phasing Out the Program

During the course of this program, a number of things have been introduced into your life that are fairly artificial — things that are unlikely to occur naturally in your family life. Examples include homework tasks, keeping records of your own and your child's behaviour, and reading the program materials. Part of finishing a program involves giving these up and going back to normal. This does not mean reverting back to all that you were doing prior to the program. The aim at this stage is to give up the artificial procedures from the program, without going back to old patterns. A number of steps are suggested to help you do this.

Put away the program materials

Put the program materials away somewhere handy so you can pull them out to look at from time to time. You may choose to mark or take out those sections of the program materials that have been the most useful so they are easy to find if you need them.

Phase out monitoring

Throughout the program, you have been asked to keep records or to monitor what you have been doing and what your child has been doing. In everyday life, most people do not keep ongoing records of their own or their child's behaviour. If you are currently keeping records of your progress, decide how well established your new behaviours are. If you feel you can continue your new behaviour without keeping a record, it is time to stop recording. If you are less certain, start to phase out the recording. Monitor your own or your child's behaviour less often, such as once a week rather than each day, and aim to phase monitoring out altogether when you feel confident of your progress.

Phase out specific strategies

Look at the types of strategies you have in place, such as behaviour charts. Decide whether these can be simplified and phased out over time. Some of the suggestions we have made, such as praising a child frequently for a particular behaviour, are most useful for changing behaviour. For maintaining behaviour, it is best to reward behaviours unpredictably from time to time, and not every time the behaviour occurs.

Make changes to behaviour charts and the use of rewards gradually. Make sure there are still plenty of rewarding things in your child's life. Behaviour problems can reappear if children do not get enough encouragement and support for appropriate behaviour.

Hold regular reviews of progress

During this program, you have attended to your family's problems on a daily or weekly basis. This can be dropped off a bit now. However, it is important to keep up with how your family is going. To pick up any problems or slip ups early, hold a progress review at least once a month.

10

Week

Update on Progress

When you began Triple P, you identified changes you would like to see in your child's behaviour as well as in your own behaviour.

EXERCISE 2 *Identifying changes that have been made*

Take a few minutes to complete the table below, outlining the changes that both you and your child have made since commencing the program. It may be helpful to look back at your goals on page 15 of this workbook.

CHANGES IN YOUR CHILD'S BEHAVIOUR	CHANGES IN YOUR OWN BEHAVIOUR

Congratulations on the changes you have made yourself and the changes you have helped your child to make.

Maintenance of Change

Obstacles to maintaining change

Here are some common reasons for not maintaining improvements made through a program like Triple P.

Family transitions

Triple P has helped you to make changes in dealing with your child's behaviour. The changes you have made are designed to suit your family as it is now. However, families change over time. They grow and develop, and change in size. Common transitions or changes families experience include the birth of a child, a parent changing employment status (e.g. rejoining the work force, taking on additional work, becoming unemployed); changes in family structure (e.g. parents separating or entering new relationships) and children growing older and moving through new developmental stages.

Children's developmental stages

The types of child behaviour problems faced by parents change as children grow older (from toddler tantrums to shyness at preschool to problems with schoolwork). Successful parenting requires flexibility over time. As the problems you encounter vary, so too will the strategies you use for dealing with these problems. This is why recommended ages are provided with the positive parenting strategies described in Sessions 3 and 4. Strategies that are useful now with your child may not be as helpful in 6 months or 6 years time. The good news is that, no matter the age of your child, the basic principles remain the same. Children will continue to respond well to consistent, effective, appropriate discipline, and will flourish and thrive in an environment that provides them with love and support.

High-risk times

There are likely to be times in your life when it will be difficult to maintain the sorts of changes you have made as part of Triple P. Research suggests that communication skills and the quality of family life tend to decrease during periods of stress. These periods of stress are known as high-risk times. For example, a death in the family, a serious illness, job loss or other major disruption, all affect how family members feel and get on with one another. These events are likely to affect things like the way parents talk with their children, their availability to others, their tolerance of misbehaviour, and their ability to plan for and deal with problems. These are the times when parents may fail to use positive parenting strategies for dealing with family problems and times when they are likely to revert to using old, ineffective approaches to child-rearing. Some common high-risk times include:

- changes in family finances
- times when parents are feeling depressed
- times of family conflict
- moving house
- renovating or building a house
- changing schools

10
Week

- death or illness in the family
- involvement in court action

Another high-risk time for many people is immediately after the end of a program such as Triple P. Unfortunately, just because the program is finished, it does not mean all the hard work is finished.

Guidelines for maintaining change

With planning and care, many of the potential problems associated with family transitions, high-risk times and changes associated with children growing older, can be avoided or minimised. There are four key steps to overcoming obstacles to maintaining change and for avoiding slip-ups.

Plan for high-risk situations

A good way to avoid problems involves planning to deal with potentially difficult times before any trouble starts. Just as you plan how to keep your child amused and out of trouble during an outing, you need to plan for future situations where problems may arise. This process can start now. Later in the session, you will spend some time thinking of possible high-risk situations that may occur in the next 6 months. Problem solving ways of dealing with these situations before they arise can help minimise problems.

Review your family's progress

If you review your family's progress on a regular basis it is more likely that you will be able to detect any problems as they arise. You will also be able to take appropriate action to prevent any lapses. Review your progress every 2 weeks at first, then once a month.

Act quickly if problems occur

It is important to take immediate action if things do start to deteriorate. You may decide to restart specific parenting strategies (such as planned activities routines or behaviour charts). It may be helpful to go back to the reading material to check strategies or look for new ideas.

Try new strategies

If existing strategies are no longer effective, try out new things. Look to what you already know — give your child lots of attention and encouragement when they are behaving well and remove your attention when they misbehave. Try to find ways of adapting strategies to new situations. Try out the new routine for 10 to 14 days, monitor how successful it is, and continue or refine the routine if necessary. Some guidelines for selecting appropriate consequences are outlined below.

- *Consequences should relate to the misbehaviour.* When consequences are directly related to misbehaviour, children learn what they have done wrong. For example, when children fight over a toy, removal of the toy from both children will help them to learn that fighting over toys is not acceptable. When you cannot think of a consequence that directly relates to the misbehaviour, consider withdrawing a privilege and explaining why you are doing so. A short withdrawal of privileges is much more effective than a long one.

Week 10

- *Consequences should provide an incentive for good behaviour.* To encourage children to behave well, they need to be given the opportunity to do so. For example, grounding a child for 3 weeks for coming home late provides no opportunity or reason for the child to behave well in the near future. A better consequence may involve, for each 5 minutes they are late, a loss of half an hour off the time they must be home the next day (e.g. not late, allowed out till 5.00 p.m. the next day; 5 minutes late, home by 4.30 p.m.; 10 minutes late, home by 4 p.m.). These consequences provide children with an incentive to try to be home on time the next day. For a child who will not turn off the television to do homework, rather than a 2 week ban from watching television, only allow television each night after homework has been completed.

- *Consequences should be appropriate to children's age and developmental stage.* Modify consequences to suit the age and abilities of your child. For example, with younger children consequences are generally shorter in duration than for older children. Older children will respond to consequences such as missing out on pocket money, extra chores, less access to computer games and shortening the length of time spent with friends after school.

- *Consequences should not threaten a child's sense of worth or self-esteem.* Punishments that are harsh, lengthy, or involve physical or verbal punishment can be damaging to your child. Many children with behaviour problems also have low self-esteem, or are anxious or depressed. Punishments can make these children feel worse about themselves. Avoid consequences which single your child out (e.g. take your child out of the room rather than dealing with a problem in front of visitors), prevent older siblings from teasing a child who is in time-out, and avoid 'telling off' or criticising your child.

- *Consequences should be enforceable.* Do not threaten a consequence unless you are prepared to carry through with it. For example, if you tell your child they cannot come along on a family day trip because they have misbehaved, then you must be prepared to follow through with this action and organise a child minder while the rest of the family goes out.

- *Consequences should be carried out immediately.* In general, children learn more quickly and can connect their actions to the consequences, if consequences are immediate. For example, if your child is disruptive during a long car trip, stop the car and put them into quiet time rather than waiting until you get to where you are going before you apply a consequence.

- *Consequences should be applied consistently.* Children are more likely to learn the results of their actions if they receive the same consequences each time a problem occurs. It is also helpful if adults respond in the same way to the same misbehaviour. To prevent children from feeling picked on, ensure all children are treated alike. Provide similar consequences for similar misbehaviour, for all children in your family. You may need to make modifications to suit the age of your child. Use consequences consistently despite excuses from children. This will discourage them from complaining and arguing with your decisions.

10
Week

Problem Solving for the Future

EXERCISE 3 *Planning for future high-risk situations*

Spend a few minutes planning possible solutions to these situations. Discuss your ideas with your practitioner and make notes if you like. What would you do if…

Your 8-year-old has been in trouble the last three weekends at football matches for yelling at his team mates and for kicking the ball into the spectators if he misses a goal or causes a penalty. You are worried he will be removed from the team if his temper outbursts continue.

Your 11-year-old is being bullied at school. Two children have started to call her names and exclude her from their games. She is coming home after school in tears and complains of feeling sick before school each day. She is also starting to call herself names (such as *Stupid* and *Ugly*) and saying she's not good at doing anything.

The summer holidays start in 3 weeks time. You will have your three school-age children home with you each day for the next 7 weeks and you expect family squabbles and complaints of being bored.

....

....

....

....

....

EXERCISE 4 *Identifying future high-risk situations*

Discuss with your practitioner any high-risk events or situations which may occur in the next 6 months (e.g. going to the dentist, starting a new school, a parent starting part-time work). List the events below.

....

....

....

....

....

....

EXERCISE 5 *Independent problem solving*

Using the blank form on page 146, devise a routine for dealing with one of the potential high-risk situations you have just identified.

PLANNED ACTIVITIES CHECKLIST

Situation: _____

Instructions: Whenever this situation occurs record Yes, No or NA (Not Applicable) for each of the steps below.

STEPS TO FOLLOW	DAY				
	STEPS COMPLETED?				
1					
2					
3					
4					
5					
6					
NUMBER OF STEPS COMPLETED CORRECTLY:					

Future Goals

EXERCISE 6 *Identifying future goals*

What further improvements would you like to see in your child's and your own behaviour? Remember to state your goals specifically (e.g. less talking back).

....

....

....

....

How could you achieve these new goals? Think about the practice exercises you could set yourself to achieve the goals stated above.

....

....

....

....

CONCLUSION

Summary of Activities

This week you have focussed on the positive changes that have occurred since you started Triple P and how you can maintain these changes. You have also thought about goals for the future and how you can achieve your goals.

■ PRACTICE EXERCISES

- Continue to practise positive parenting strategies.
- Continue to develop and implement planned activities routines for high-risk situations.
- Write down your goals for the coming week.

....

....

....

....

10
Week

> List any material you feel you need to review this week.
>
> ....
>
> ....
>
> ....
>
> ....

Congratulations

You have now completed Self-Help Triple P. Thank you for maintaining your interest and motivation throughout the program. We hope you have enjoyed participating in the program and are enjoying the benefits of positive parenting. Keep up the good work. As your child continues to grow, different situations and new problems are bound to arise. Refer back to your workbook and other Triple P resources at any time to review the strategies you have learnt or to look up guidelines for dealing with a new problem behaviour. If you have any concerns in the future about your child's progress or any family issues, seek professional advice. Thank you for participating in Triple P. We hope you found it a worthwhile experience.

Where To From Here?

If you have completed Self-Help Triple P and feel that you are experiencing difficulties with your child's behaviour, your own feelings or your relationship with your partner, be prepared to seek professional help. Contact your family doctor, child health nurse, kindergarten or school teacher to find out where further help is available, or look up psychology services in the telephone book.

Answers to Exercises

EXERCISE 6 *Keeping track*

Suggested monitoring forms for:

- How often a child bites others.

A behaviour diary could be used if the biting occurs less than about five times per day, otherwise a tally sheet may be more appropriate. A parent may choose to complete a tally sheet as well as complete a row on a behaviour diary for one episode of biting per day to help find out more about the triggers and consequences of the biting. A duration record would not be appropriate given that biting can occur in an instant. Unless the biting occurs more than 15 times a day, a time sample would also be inappropriate.

- How long a child takes to settle when left with other carers.

A duration record would show how long a child protests or cries when left with others. The carer would need to complete this record as the parent will not be present. Since the behaviour only occurs once a day, neither a tally sheet nor time sample would be appropriate. A behaviour diary may be used to help find out more about the triggers and consequences of the protesting.

- How often a child whines, particularly in the afternoon before dinner.

Given that whining is a behaviour that seems to go on and on, it is not always possible to tell when one incident of whining stops and another one starts. Therefore a time sample would be most appropriate. One option involves breaking the period between 3:30pm and 6:00pm into 15 minute intervals and recording the presence or absence of whining in each 15 minute interval. If the whining occurs often, a tally sheet and behaviour diary would not be appropriate. Also a duration record is unlikely to be appropriate as whining is often cyclic rather than continuous.

- How often a child is destructive.

Given that an incidence of destructive behaviour is easily observable, a tally sheet or behaviour diary would be most appropriate. It is unlikely that destructiveness would occur often enough to warrant a time sample or long enough to warrant a duration record.

- How often a child answers back or uses a negative tone of voice.

Depending on how often this behaviour occurs, a behaviour diary (less than 5 times per day) or frequency tally (up to 15 times per day) or time sample (several times per hour) may be used. A duration record is not likely to be helpful for this behaviour as talking back often comes and goes quickly.

WEEK 2

EXERCISE 8 *Incidental teaching*

- When your child asks you questions, particularly the common *Why?* Questions (e.g. *Why is the moon round tonight?*).

For *Why?* questions, you could say something like *Hmmm, is the moon always round?* or *Why do you think the moon is round? What other shapes can the moon be?*

- When your child mispronounces a word (e.g. *sgetti* instead of *spaghetti*).

When your child mispronounces a word you could say *Yes Sam, we're having spaghetti for dinner. Spag-het-ti… That's a good try.*

- When your child is engaged in an activity and wants to show you something (e.g. *Come and look at my painting!*).

You could say something like *That's a great picture. Tell me about your drawing… What's this person doing? Where are they going?*

- When your child is frustrated with an activity and asks for help (e.g., *I can't do this puzzle!*).

You could say *What's the problem? Oh, you can't find the next piece for the puzzle. What colours would be on the missing piece? What shape would the missing piece be?… OK let's look for a piece with three connectors and pink around the edge.*

EXERCISE **3** *Ideas for using planned ignoring*

- For which minor problem behaviours could you use planned ignoring?

Planned ignoring is best used for minor problem behaviour that is aimed at getting attention from parents. Example minor problem behaviours include whining, pulling faces, making silly noises and using rude words.

- When do you stop ignoring a minor problem behaviour?

Only stop ignoring when the problem behaviour has stopped (and then praise your child for stopping the problem behaviour) or the behaviour has changed in nature to become more serious, such as being aggressive and hitting out. In this case, other strategies such as clear, calm instructions, logical consequences, quiet time and time-out should be used to deal with the serious problem behaviour (see Week 3).

- What would stop you from using planned ignoring?

Many parents find it hard to ignore pestering or whining. Others are very conscious of being watched by others (e.g. extended family or while out in the community) and find it too stressful not to intervene more actively with their child. If either is the case, it is best not to use planned ignoring. It will only work if you can ignore the minor problem behaviour until it stops.

EXERCISE **4** *Ideas for giving clear, calm instructions*

- It's time for your child's dinner.

Heidi, it's time for dinner, come to the table now please or *Go and sit at the table for dinner now please Heidi.* (Repeat once as this is an instruction to start a new task)

- Your child is jumping on the couch.

Mark, stop jumping on the couch. Please sit down on the couch. (Do not repeat as this is an instruction to stop a problem behaviour)

- Your child's toys are scattered on the floor.

Billy, please go and put your toys in the box now or *Billy, it's pack up time. Help me put the toys in the box now please.* (Repeat once as this is an instruction to start a new task)

- Your child is interrupting your telephone call.

Helen, stop pulling Mummy's dress. If you want Mummy, say "excuse me" and wait until I am free. (Do not repeat as this is an instruction to stop a problem behaviour)

- It's time for your child to get ready to go out.

Lucas, it's time to get ready for preschool. Come and get your sandals on please or *Lucas, go and get your kindy bag now please.* (Repeat once as this is an instruction to start a new task)

Avoid using the following words when giving instructions:

Would you like to…?

I want you to…

Can you…?

It would make me happy if you would…

Do you want to…?

These are all examples of vague instructions as they do not clearly tell the child exactly what they need to do. When instructions are phrased as questions, children have a choice and can say *No*. Instructions that are merely statements of what parents would like or want do not suggest action.

EXERCISE 5 *Choosing logical consequences*

- Your child is playing with their drink at the dinner table.

Remove the drink for 5 to 30 minutes (e.g. *You are still playing with your drink, so the drink goes away for 5 minutes*).

- Your child is playing roughly with a toy.

Remove the toy for 5 to 30 minutes (e.g. *You are playing too roughly with your toy, I will have to put it away for 10 minutes*).

- Your child is wandering away from you on a walk.

Hold your child's hand for 1 or 2 minutes or for 10 to 20 steps (e.g. *You are walking too far away from me, now you must hold my hand for 20 steps*).

- Your child is playing dangerously on the swings.

Bring your child off the swings for 5 to 30 minutes (e.g. *You are not sitting and holding on carefully like I asked you to, so now you must stay off the swing for 5 minutes*).

- Your child is drawing on the wall.

Remove the pencils for 5 to 30 minutes or have your child clean the wall if they are able (e.g. *You are still drawing on the wall, so I'm putting the pencils away for 10 minutes*).

Use consequences of 5 to 10 minutes for toddlers and preschool-age children. Longer consequences (up to 30 minutes) can be used for primary school-age children.

EXERCISE 6 *Preparing to use quiet time*

- What space in your home could be used for quiet time?

Any space on the edge of an activity where a problem has occurred (e.g. a chair in the kitchen, lounge room or family room).

- What can you say to your child as you take them to quiet time?

You have not done as I asked, now you must go to quiet time.

- What can you say to your child as you put them in quiet time?

You need to sit here and be quiet for 2 minutes before you can come out.

- How long will your child need to be quiet in quiet time?

One minute for children up to 2 years old; 2 minutes for 3–5 year-olds; and a maximum of 5 minutes for children between 5 and 10 years of age.

- When can you talk to your child again?

After they have been quiet for the set time. Start timing once they are quiet, not just when you put them into quiet time. Do not talk to your child while they are in quiet time.

- What can you say to your child when quiet time is over?

Thank you for being quiet, you can come out now. Catch your child behaving well and praise them as soon as possible after quiet time.

- What can you do if your child is not quiet within 10 seconds or does not stay seated in quiet time?

Allow 10 seconds for your child to settle down when you put them in quiet time. If they are not quiet within 10 seconds, tell them what they have done wrong and take them to time-out — *You are not being quiet in quiet time, now you must go to time-out.* If your child does not stay in the quiet time area, tell them what they have done wrong and take them to time-out.

EXERCISE 7 *Preparing to use time-out*

- What room or space could you use for time-out in your home?

The bathroom, laundry or spare room. Make sure the room you use is safe (i.e. child-proofed).

- What can you say to your child as you take them to time-out?

You have not done as I asked, now you must go to time-out.

- What can you say to your child as you put them in time-out?

You must be quiet for 2 minutes before you can come out.

- How long will your child need to be quiet in time-out?

One minute for 2 year-olds; 2 minutes for 3–5 year-olds; and a maximum of 5 minutes for children between 5 and 10 years of age.

- When can you talk to your child again?

After they have been quiet for the set time. Start timing once they are quiet, not just when you put them into time-out. Do not talk to your child while they are in time-out and do not let them out if they are still calling out or making noise.

- What can you say to your child when time-out is over?

Thank you for being quiet, you can come out now. Catch your child behaving well and praise them as soon as possible after time-out.

- What could you do if your child refused to come out of time-out when it was over?

Tell your child that time-out is over and suggest something else for them to do. If they refuse to come out, leave them to come out when they are ready. Do not give them any attention while they stay in the time-out room. Watch for when your child gets involved in an activity and praise them.

- What could you do if your child made a mess in the time-out room?

Stay calm and wait for your child to be quiet for the set time in time-out. In a calm voice, tell your child when time-out is over and that they can come out when the mess has been cleaned up. Make sure your expectations about your child's ability to clean up are realistic — do not expect perfection. Once the room is reasonably tidy, your child can come out.

- What could you do if your child came out of time-out before their time was up?

Time-out is controlled by you, the parent, not your child. You must decide when your child can come out. If your child comes out before the time is up, put them back in time-out and make sure they cannot let themselves out.

- What could happen if you threaten to use time-out with your child?

They may learn to comply only with a threat rather than with your instruction. If time-out is not used consistently every time serious misbehaviour occurs, the misbehaviour is likely to get worse.

- What could happen if you let your child out of time-out while they are still upset?

They may learn to get upset and cry and scream (i.e. escalate) to get out of time-out. Also, more misbehaviour is likely to occur if your child comes out of time-out before they have calmed down. To break the escalation trap, children need to learn that they will only get attention when they are behaving well and that when they misbehave, attention is removed.

Worksheets

It is intended that you will make multiple copies of the following worksheets to use with your workbook. Remember to keep the originals so you can make additional copies as required.

BEHAVIOUR DIARY

Instructions: List the problem behaviour, when and where it occurred and what happened before and after the event.

Problem Behaviour: _____

Day: _____

PROBLEM EVENT	WHEN AND WHERE DID IT OCCUR?	WHAT OCCURRED BEFORE THE EVENT?	WHAT OCCURRED AFTER THE EVENT?	OTHER COMMENTS

TALLY SHEET

Instructions: Write the day in the first column, then place a tick in the successive square each time the behaviour occurs on that day. Record the total number of episodes for each day in the end column.

Behaviour: _____

Starting Date: _____

DAY	1	2	3	4	5	6	7	8	9	10	11	12	13	14	15	TOTAL

DURATION RECORD

Instructions: Write the day in the first column, then for each separate occurrence of the target behaviour, record how long it lasted in seconds, minutes or hours. Total the times at the end of each day.

Behaviour: _____   Starting Date: _____

DAY	SUCCESSIVE EPISODES										TOTAL
	1	2	3	4	5	6	7	8	9	10	

TIME SAMPLE

Instructions: Place a tick in the square for the corresponding time period if the target behaviour has occurred at least once.

Behaviour: _____   Starting Date: _____

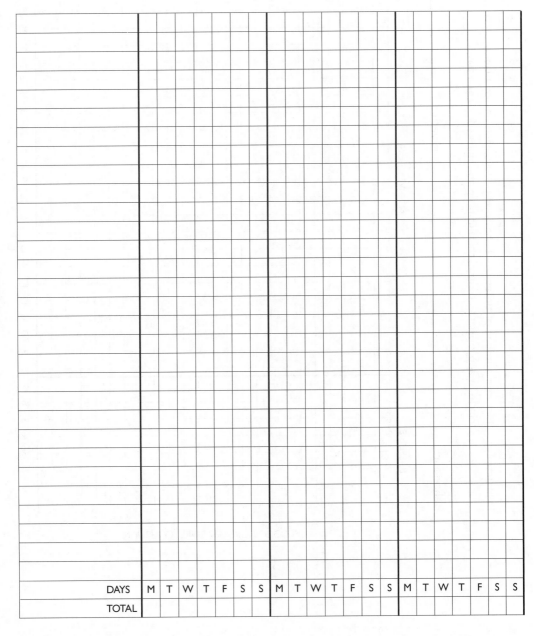

DAYS	M	T	W	T	F	S	S	M	T	W	T	F	S	S	M	T	W	T	F	S	S
TOTAL																					

TIME OF DAY

BEHAVIOUR GRAPH

Instructions: Plot the number of times the behaviour occurs each day by placing a cross or circle in appropriate column, then join up the marks for each day.

Behaviour: _____   Month: _____

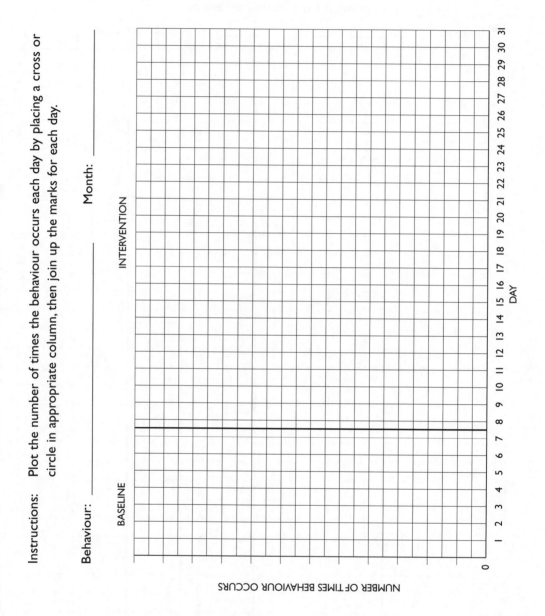

BASELINE   INTERVENTION

NUMBER OF TIMES BEHAVIOUR OCCURS

0 1 2 3 4 5 6 7 8 9 10 11 12 13 14 15 16 17 18 19 20 21 22 23 24 25 26 27 28 29 30 31

DAY

CHECKLIST FOR PROMOTING CHILDREN'S DEVELOPMENT

Choose two of the strategies discussed in Week 2 which you would like to practise with your child over the next week. Be as specific as possible (e.g. one goal may be to use descriptive praise statements with your child at least five times per day). Use the table below to record whether you reached your goals each day. Comment on what went well and list any problems that occurred.

GOAL 1: ....

....

GOAL 2: ....

....

DAY	GOAL 1 Y/N	GOAL 2 Y/N	COMMENTS
1			
2			
3			
4			
5			
6			
7			

Instructions: Make a note of the day, the problem behaviour, when and where it occurred, and the total length of time your child was in time-out.

Set time for time-out: ☐ 2 minutes ☐ 3 minutes ☐ 4 minutes ☐ 5 minutes

DAY	PROBLEM BEHAVIOUR	WHEN AND WHERE IT OCCURRED	LENGTH OF TIME-OUT

PRACTICE TASK CHECKLIST

Note down your goals for the practice task. Be as specific as possible (e.g. one goal may be to use descriptive praise statements with your child at least three times). Use the table below to record whether you reached your goals. Comment on what went well and list any problems that occurred.

GOAL 1:
....

....

GOAL 2:
....

....

GOAL 3:
....

....

	GOAL ACHIEVED? Y/N	COMMENTS
GOAL 1		
GOAL 2		
GOAL 3		

PLANNED ACTIVITIES ROUTINE

Identify the high-risk situation

....

Specify details for a practice session (when, where, who should be present)

....

....

....

List any advance planning or preparation

....

....

....

Decide on rules

....

....

....

Select engaging activities

....

....

....

List rewards for appropriate behaviour

....

....

....

List consequences for misbehaviour

....

....

....

Note any goals from the follow-up discussion

....

....

....

PLANNED ACTIVITIES CHECKLIST

Situation: _____

Instructions: Whenever this situation occurs record Yes, No or NA (Not Applicable) for each of the steps below.

STEPS TO FOLLOW	DAY				
	STEPS COMPLETED?				
1					
2					
3					
4					
5					
6					
NUMBER OF STEPS COMPLETED CORRECTLY:					

NOTES